WARD'S DAILY ALMANAC PRESENTS

THE BOOK OF APRIL

Compiled by W.B. Ward

Edited by Vickie L. Parrish

ISBN 1453748237 ISBN-13 978-1453748237

For Jim and April.

Table of Contents

FORWARD

Contrary to what one may believe from reading this book (or any one of the twelve books in its series), I have not always had a love for history. In fact, if any of my history teachers knew that I had taken on this project, they would be stunned into permanent insanity! As my son has reminded me on more than one occasion, there was so little history to study when I was a student that I had no excuse whatsoever!

It wasn't until I became a broadcaster that I first began to be intrigued by the paths that many had taken through time. At first, I became somewhat of a trivia buff. At the time it was considered quite appropriate for disc jockeys to come up with entertaining trivia questions in order to give away various trinkets to adoring listeners. One station where I had worked (KAKC; Tulsa, OK) had a morning man ("Morning Mouth McCarthy") who had a daily presentation of "Little-Less-Known-and-Little-Less-Cared-For-Facts." This was the genesis of my curiosity.

Of course this led to the eventual purchase of the popular game "Trivial Pursuit." It was through this game where I really began learning about history and its importance to everyday life.

Although the game certainly had its share of errors (as in the case of many historical collections), it still fed my curiosity and developed a philosophy of learning that I wished I had possessed while I was still in school.

Among my lessons, I learned that history truly is a living thing. It began the second I was born and will continue long after I've gone. History is simply a collection of footprints left by countless individuals as they walked over the sands of life's many beaches. Some footprints are larger than others and some are much clearer; but all footprints move in the same direction: from start to finish.

Some footprints have been declared more important than others, but that's where I tend to take issue with many educators. Yes, I see the importance of events like the signing of the Declaration of Independence, the attack on Pearl Harbor, and Columbus' famous trips. However, what I believe are important are the more mundane events of time; the invention of the beer pump handle, the first soda jerk, the day color television first became available, and so forth. The events covered in textbooks are truly important, but it is the trivial that truly make us who we have become and colors our world.

My sources of information are as varied as the facts themselves. Some of the events I found in newspapers, some in book and some in documentaries and on rare occasions, I was actually around to see the incident take place first-hand. Of course, the Internet has always provided an ample amount of information and I have verified every tidbit of information as much as humanly possible. That being said, I feel the need to make one thing abundantly clear: this body of work should only be treated as light reading. I offer it for entertainment purposes (i.e., "water cooler chat") only. Occasional, hopefully rare, errors may be present.

It is my sincerest wish that people who stumble across this book will place it in a well-known spot in their bookcase and refer to it often. It is interesting to see what happened on our various red-letter days, and to see who shares the same birthdays. Sometimes it is not enough to know the how and why, but it is occasionally important to also know the when.

This is but one of my footprints.

W.B. Ward

ABOUT THE AUTHOR

Having worked as a mentalist, W. B. Ward discovered that his effects were often based on tricks used by con men to bilk honest people from their hard-earned money. Using his craft as a springboard, he began researching various schemes to defraud unwitting victims, and he has compiled his findings into a book called Brother Can You Spare a Dime? And Other Popular Cons. In it, he reveals a myriad of

W.B. Ward

swindles, along with suggested defenses against each con. (Sadly, however, this book is currently out of print.)

Born in 1958, W. B. Ward has worked in various fields of the entertainment industry including: music, radio, television, theatre, concerts, carnivals, professional wrestling, and others.

In radio he has worked in stations coast to coast including (but not limited to): 97.5 KMOD; 101.5 the Beat; 92.1 KISS FM; KOOL 106.1; KAKC AM 1300; AM 1430 the Buzz; KMUS; KRLQ; KBIX; KGNX-TV; KRRG-FM; KRKC-FM; KNIC; and KVOO. His television credits include KGNS-TV; KOKI Fox 23; KLDO-TV; KOTV; KTUL; KJRH; ABC's *That's Incredible*; Westwood One's *PM Magazine*; and he was invited to perform on NBC's *Phenomenon*. W. B. Ward currently writes and produces a daily 2-minute feature, *Wards Daily Almanac*, which airs on stations around the country.

Playing over 30 instruments, he is also an accomplished musician. His love of performing, combined with his love for music, encouraged him into the studio where he has recorded (and is currently recording) a number of CDs.

If you would like to book W. B. Ward as a motivational speaker at your next event, meeting, or convention, send us an email to check for availability. Email all enquiries to: info@wbward.com.

For more information on W. B. Ward's books, CDs, radio programs, or personal appearances, please visit his website at: www.wbward.com.

April: The Beginning

Openings. Trees begin stretching their branches toward the heavens and their fingers begin to explode in foliage garnished with the blossoms of their fruit. Stems begin pushing through the soil reaching upwards like their stately tree-brethren while colorful petals begin painting the landscape creating nature's graceful mosaic of spring. Thus is the month that marks openings: the month of April.

Many small animals that spent the winter months in hibernation come back to life during this month of regeneration and begin to re-populate the floor of the forest. Birds, once absent from gray winter nights, become ornaments on tree branches and fill the air with song.

It is by no means a mere accident that the believed etymology of this month comes from the Latin word *aperire*, which means, "to open." Like the opening of the colorful gardens, April brings with it the opening of warmth and the season of celebrating the great outdoors.

Timing, as they say, is everything, and April seems to time itself after two months. It begins on the same day of the week as July (except in Leap Years when it mimics January), and it always ends on the same day of the week as December.

People born in April are born under the sign Aries until April 20th when the astrological sign becomes Taurus. These people are described as active and energetic, and are people who display a strong mentality.

The traditional birthstone for April is the diamond, and the birth flower is usually listed as the Daisy or the Sweet Pea.

APRIL 1ST

BIRTHDAYS FOR APRIL 1ST

1873 Sergei Rachmaninoff; composer, pianist

1883 Lon Chaney Sr.; actor

1928 George Grizzard; actor

1929 Jane Powell (Suzanne Burce); actress

1929 Bo Schembechler, Jr.; football coach

1930 Grace Lee Whitney; American actress

1932 Gordon Jump; actor

1932 Debbie Reynolds; American actress

1934 Jim Ed (James Edward) Brown; singer

1938 Ali MacGraw; actress

1942 Phil Margo; singer

1944 Rusty Staub; baseball

1945 John Barbata; musician, drummer

1947 Dwight David Eisenhower II; lawyer, author

1948 Willie Montañez; baseball

1952 Billy Currie; musician, synthesizer player, keyboardist, violinist

1952 Annette O'Toole; actress

1961 Mark White; musician, guitarist

1961 Susan Boyle; Scottish singer and Britain's Got Talent contestant

1964 Kevin Duckworth; basketball

1980 Randy Orton; American professional wrestler

EVENTS FOR APRIL 1*st*

1621 - The first colonial treaty with Native Americans was signed between Massasoit, chief of the Wampanoags, and English pilgrims on behalf of King James I.

Title Page for *Household Words* with the first installment of the serial "Hard Times" by Charles Dickens. Public domain.

1789 - The United States House of Representatives was able to transact business when a quorum of its members was present for the first time.

1826 - Samuel Morey of Oxford, New Hampshire, patented the internal combustion engine.

1854 – *Hard Times* was first published as a serial in Charles Dickens' magazine, *Household Words*.

1873 – The British steamer RMS *Atlantic*, a

transatlantic ocean liner of the White Star Line (yes, the same company who owned the *Titanic*) sank off Nova Scotia, killing 547.

1877 - Ignoring the taunts of fellow miners who said he would only find his own tombstone, prospector Edward Schieffelin began his search for silver. Later that year Schieffelin was not only alive and well, but he had found one of the richest silver veins in the West. He named it the Tombstone Lode. It is now known as Tombstone, Arizona.

1917 - Composer of popular piano rag tunes Scott Joplin died.

1918 – The Royal Air Force in Britain was created by the merger of the Royal Flying Corps and the Royal Naval Air Service.

1924 - Adolf Hitler was sentenced to five years in jail for his participation in the "Beer Hall Putsch." However, he spent only nine months in jail, during which he wrote *Mein Kampf*.

1931 - The Chattanooga Baseball Club signed pitcher Jackie Mitchell who, at 19 years old, became the first woman in organized baseball.

1933 - In Germany, the state ordered a one-day boycott of businesses belonging to Jewish people and seized their bank accounts.

1941 - On New York City's FM radio station W71NY, the first contract for advertising on a commercial FM station began.

1946 - An undersea earthquake off the Alaskan coast triggered a massive tsunami that killed 165 people in Hawaii. Some people ignored the early reports thinking that it was an April Fools' prank. Unfortunately, it was all too real.

1954 – President Dwight D. Eisenhower authorized the creation of the United States Air Force Academy in Colorado.

More than 1,300 basic cadets salute during the ceremonial Oath of Office formation on June 26, 2009. The Cadet Chapel is in the background. Public domain.

1955 - After six years on NBC-TV, *One Man's Family* was seen on for the final time. The radio show of the same name continued until 1959.

1956 – Starting as a reporter, Chet Huntley began his news career with NBC with a program called *Outlook*.

1957 - The BBC broadcast a documentary that showed how Italians harvested spaghetti from trees. Many viewers believed the hoax and attempted to purchase spaghetti seeds from their local seed stores.

1960 – Tiros I, the world's first meteorological satellite which transmitted cloud cover pictures, was launched from the United States.

1963 - The television soap opera *General Hospital* began its long run on ABC-TV. (It was still running as of this writing, and according to the *Guinness Book of World Records* holds the title as the longest-running American soap opera.)

1963 – The television soap opera *The Doctors* began its 20-year run on NBC-TV.

1965 - King Hussein of Jordan appointed his younger brother Prince Hassan as his heir.

1970 – President Richard Nixon signed the Public Health Cigarette Smoking Act into law which required the Surgeon General's warnings on tobacco products and banned cigarette advertisements on television and radio in the United States. The law went into effect January 1, 1971.

1973 – The Value Added Tax (a tax on the "value added" to a product or material, from an accounting view, at each stage of its manufacture or distribution) became operative in the United Kingdom.

1976 – Apple Inc. was formed by Steve Jobs and Steve Wozniak. The Apple I, their first computer, went on sale in July 1976 and was market-priced at $666.66.

1976 – The first half of *Helter Skelter* aired on CBS-TV, and the second half was broadcast the following evening. The movie was based upon the murders committed by the Charles Manson Family.

1979 – Iran became an Islamic Republic by a 98% vote, officially overthrowing the Shah.

1984 – Just one day before his 45th birthday, pop singer, songwriter, and musician Marvin Gaye, Jr. was shot to death by his father.

1987 - Steve Newman became the first man to walk around the world alone. It took him 4 years, and countless pairs of shoes to finish.

1993 – As an April Fools' joke, DJ Dave Rickards told listeners of KGB-FM in San Diego that the Space Shuttle *Discovery* had been diverted from Edwards Air Force Base and would be landing at Montgomery Field, a small municipal airport with a 4,577 foot runway. Thousands of people went to the airport to watch the purported landing, causing traffic jams throughout Kearny Mesa. Moreover, there wasn't even a shuttle in orbit at the time.

1996 - In Japan, the world's largest bank at that time was created when the merger of the Mitsubishi Bank and the Bank of Tokyo was completed.

1996 - Taco Bell took out a full-page ad in the *New York Times* announcing that the taco chain had actually purchased the Liberty Bell. Claiming that they bought it to reduce the national debt, they re-named it the Taco Liberty Bell. It was, of course, an April Fools' Day prank.

1998 - Burger King advertised a left-handed hamburger. According to their ad, the burger was designed specifically for left-handed people, as it would only drip its juices from the right-hand side. It was again, another April Fools' Day prank.

2008 - Today is when the BBC reported the story of a rare flock of flying penguins in Antarctica that migrated from the South Pole to the Amazon Rain Forest. In case you were wondering, penguins don't fly.

APRIL 2ⁿᵈ

BIRTHDAYS FOR APRIL 2ⁿᵈ

1725 Giovanni Casanova; writer

1805 Hans Christian Andersen; author

1875 Walter Chrysler; auto manufacturer

1908 Buddy Ebsen; actor

1914 Sir Alec Guinness; Academy Award-winning actor

1920 Jack Webb; director, actor

1924 Bobby Ávila; baseball

1939 Marvin Gaye; singer

1941 Dr. Demento (Barret Eugene Hansen); American radio personality

1942 Leon Russell; singer; songwriter

1945 Linda Hunt; Academy Award-winning actress

1945 Reggie (Carl Reginald) Smith; baseball

1945 Don Sutton; baseball

1947 Emmylou Harris; grammy Award-winning singer

1953 Pamela Reed; actress

1953 Debralee Scott; actress

1961 Christopher Meloni; actor

1961 Keren Woodward; English singer (Bananarama)

1965 Rodney King; American victim of police brutality

1986 Lee DeWyze; Singer, American Idol winner in 2010

EVENTS FOR APRIL 2nd

1513 – Juan Ponce de León set foot on Florida, becoming the first European known to do so.

1792 - Congress approved the Coinage Act, authorizing the first United States Mint.

1801 - The Danish fleet was destroyed in the Napoleonic Wars by the British under Admiral Nelson at the Battle of Copenhagen.

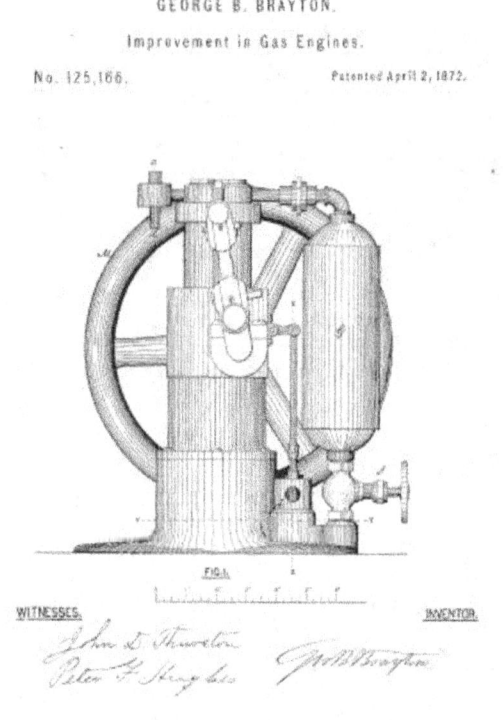

First page of original patent drawings for the gas-powered streetcar. Public domain.

1860 - The first Italian Parliament met at Turin.

1872 – G.B. Brayton, of Boston, Massachusetts, received patent #125,166 for the gas-powered streetcar.

1889 - Charles Hall patented aluminum.

1902 – The "Electric Theatre," the first full-time movie theater in the United States, opened in Los Angeles, California.

1944 - The Soviet Union announced that its troops had crossed the Prut River and entered Romania.

1947 - The United Nations Security Council voted to appoint the United States as trustee for former Japanese-held Pacific Islands.

1951 - General Dwight Eisenhower assumed command of all allied armies in Western Mediterranean area and Europe.

1956 - Two successful daytime dramas premiered on CBS-TV: *The Edge of Night* and *As the World Turns*; both of which were the first daytime dramas to debut in the 30-minute format.

1969 - The NBA's Milwaukee Bucks signed Lew Alcindor (who later changed his name to Kareem Abdul-Jabar) for a reported $1.4 million five-year contract.

1972 - Actor Burt Reynolds appeared naked in *Cosmopolitan* magazine. The issue became an instant collector's item and an additional 700,000 copies were printed.

1972 – Actor Charlie Chaplin returned to the United States for the first time since being labeled a communist during the Red Scare in the early 1950s.

1974 – Millions of television viewers watching the live *Academy Awards* ceremony saw a naked man named Robert Opel "streak" across the stage. Without missing a beat, host David Niven said, "Isn't it fascinating to think that probably the only laugh that man will ever get in his life is by stripping off and showing his shortcomings?" (By the way, the award for "Best Picture" that evening went to *The Sting*.)

1975 – Construction of the CN Tower was completed in Toronto, Ontario, Canada. It reached 1,815.4 feet, becoming the world's tallest free-standing structure to date.

1978 – CBS-TV's drama *Dallas* made its national debut.

1982 - Argentina invaded the Falkland Islands and overthrew the British administration; Britain responded by sending a task force to retake the islands.

1989 – Soviet leader Mikhail Gorbachev arrived in Havana, Cuba, to meet with Fidel Castro in an attempt to mend strained relations.

1990 - According to the Reuters news agency, Saddam Hussein said, "I swear to God we will let our fire eat half of Israel if it tries to wage anything against Iraq."

The FBI Mugshot of Gotti taken in 1990. Public domain.

1992 – Mafia boss John Gotti, nicknamed "Teflon Don" after emerging unscathed from previous trials, was convicted of murder and racketeering. He was later sentenced to life in prison. CAPTION: The FBI Mugshot of Gotti taken in 1990. Public domain.

2002 – Israeli forces surrounded the Church of the Nativity in Bethlehem into which armed Palestinians had retreated. A siege ensued.

2004 – Islamist terrorists involved in the March 11, 2004 Madrid attacks attempted to bomb the Spanish high-speed train near Madrid. Their attack was thwarted.

2006 – Over 60 tornadoes broke out; hardest hit was Tennessee with 29 people killed.

APRIL 3rd

BIRTHDAYS FOR APRIL 3rd

1783 Washington Irving; author

1837 John Burroughs; author

1898 George Jessel; comedian, actor

1898 Henry Luce; editor and publisher

1904 Sally Rand; American burlesque dancer

1907 Iron Eyes Cody; American actor

1923 Jan Sterling; actress

1922 Doris Day (Kappelhoff); singer

1924 Marlon Brando; Academy Award-winning actor

1926 Gus Grissom; American astronaut

1928 Don Gibson; singer

1930 Helmut Kohl; Chancellor of Germany

1934 Jane Goodall; anthropologist

1942 Billy Joe Royal; American singer

1942 Wayne Newton; singer

1943 Jonathan Lynn; actor

1943 Doreen Tracey; English-born Mouseketeer

1944 Tony Orlando (Michael Anthony Orlando Cassevitis); singer

1945 Bernard Parent; hockey

1951 Mel Schacher; musician, bassist

1956 Ray Combs; American game show host and comedian

1958 Alec Baldwin; actor

1959 David Hyde Pierce; actor

1961 Eddie Murphy; comedian

1969 Lance Storm; Canadian wrestler

1971 Picabo Street; Olympic skier

1972 Jennie Garth; actress

1975 Michael Olowokandi; basketball

EVENTS FOR APRIL 3rd

1559 - Philip II of Spain and Henry II of France signed the Treaty of Cateau-Cambresis in France, ending almost 60 years of war.

1721 - Sir Robert Walpole was appointed first Lord of the Treasury and Chancellor of the Exchequer, effectively Britain's first prime minister.

1776 - Harvard College awarded the first honorary Doctor of Laws degree to George Washington.

1829 - James Carrington of Connecticut patented the coffee mill. Milling devices had been available for hundreds of years, dating back to the Greek and Roman Empires, and several versions of coffee mills had been granted in the United States. Today was Mr. Carrington's turn.

1860 – The first successful United States Pony Express run began. The first route

One of the first recruiting posters used in 1860. Public domain.

was from Saint Joseph, Missouri to Sacramento, California

1882 - After more than 15 years of robbing banks, outlaw Jesse James was shot in the back in St. Joseph, Missouri by Robert Ford, one of his own gang.

1885 – Gottlieb Daimler was granted a German patent for his engine design.

1888 – The first of eleven unsolved brutal murders of women committed in or near the impoverished Whitechapel district in the East End of London occurred. These were the murders attributed to an unidentified character only referred to as "Jack the Ripper."

Portrait of Oscar Wilde taken in 1882 by Napoleon Sarony. Public domain.

1895 – Trial of the libel case instigated by Oscar Wilde began, eventually resulting in his imprisonment on charges of homosexuality.

1913 - English suffragette Emmeline Pankhurst was found guilty of bombing the home of David Lloyd George, the Chancellor of the Exchequer, and sentenced to three years in prison.

1917 – Vladimir Lenin arrived in Russia from exile, marking the beginning of Bolshevik leadership in the Russian Revolution.

1922 – Joseph Stalin became the first General Secretary of the Communist Party of the Soviet Union.

1929 – RMS *Queen Mary* was ordered from John Brown & Company Shipbuilding and Engineering by Cunard Line.

The *Queen Mary* in permanent dock as a tourist attraction. Photo taken by Mike Fernwood. Used by permission.

1933 - First Lady Eleanor Roosevelt told newspaper reporters beer would be served at the White House once it became legal to do so.

1936 – Bruno Richard Hauptmann was executed for the kidnapping and death of Charles Augustus Lindbergh II, the baby son of pilot Charles Lindbergh.

1941 - The British evacuated Benghazi in the face of the German advance in World War II.

1942 – Japanese forces began an assault on the United States and Filipino troops on the Bataan Peninsula.

1946 – Japanese Lt. General Masaharu Homma was executed in the Philippines for leading the Bataan Death March.

1948 - *The Louisiana Hayride* radio program premiered on KWKH-AM. This program launched the careers not only of several country-music giants, but also of a young singer named Elvis Presley.

1948 - United States President Harry S Truman signed the Marshall plan, which allocated $6 billion in overseas economic aid.

1949 - Transjordan signed an armistice with the newly founded state of Israel.

1949 - Dean Martin and Jerry Lewis made their radio debut in an NBC program called, appropriately, *Dean Martin and Jerry Lewis* that ran until 1952.

1953 - *TV Guide* was first published. In its first year, the publication reached a circulation of 1,500,000 readers.

1955 – The American Civil Liberties Union announced it would defend Allen Ginsberg's poem "Howl" against obscenity charges.

1955 - Fred Astaire made his television debut on *The Toast of the Town*, hosted by Ed Sullivan.

1962 - Race jockey Eddie Arcaro announced his retirement with 4,779 victories, for total winnings of $30,039,543.

1968 - Stanley Kubrick's science fiction masterpiece, *2001: A Space Odyssey*, opened in United States theaters.

1973 – The first portable cell phone call was made in New York City.

1974 – "The Super Outbreak," the biggest tornado outbreak in recorded history, occurred. No less than 163 tornadoes ripped through 13 states, killing 315, and injuring nearly 5,500.

1975 – Russia's Anatoly Karpov was proclaimed world chess champion after American Bobby Fischer refused to defend his title.

1982 - The United States Security Council voted 10-1 in favor of Resolution 502, demanding withdrawal of Argentine forces from the Falkland Islands.

1982 - John Chancellor left his position as anchor of *The NBC Nightly News*. Roger Mudd and Tom Brokaw took over as co-anchors.

1985 – Hollywood, California's famed "Brown Derby" restaurant on Wilshire

Boulevard closed after a 57 years.

1994 - After 37 years with CBS, newsman Charles Kuralt retired.

The original Brown Derby on Wilshire Boulevard. Photo by Chalmers Butterfield. Used by permission.

1996 – Suspected "Unabomber" Theodore Kaczynski was arrested at his cabin in Montana, United States. He began his life as a child prodigy; he excelled academically from an early age. Kaczynshi was accepted into Harvard University at the age of 16, where he earned an undergraduate degree, and later earned a PhD in mathematics from the University of Michigan. He now spends his life behind bars as he was sentenced to life in prison without the possibility of parole.

1996 - A plane carrying United States Commerce Secretary, Ron Brown, crashed in Croatia, killing all 29 passengers and six crew members aboard.

2000 – Microsoft was ruled to have violated United States antitrust laws by keeping "an oppressive thumb" on its competitors.

2004 – Islamic terrorists involved in the March 11, 2004 Madrid attacks were trapped by the police in their apartment. The terrorists avoided arrest by committing suicide.

2007 – A French TGV train set an official new world speed record at 357.2 mph.

2008 – ATA Airlines, once one of the 10 largest U.S. passenger airlines and largest charter airline, filed for bankruptcy for the second time in 5 years and ceases all operations.

2008 – SWAT team members raided the YFZ Ranch in Eldorado, Texas after getting a call claiming underage marriages and child abuse were going on inside the ranch.

APRIL 4th

BIRTHDAYS FOR APRIL 4th

1821 Linus Yale, Jr.; inventor

1895 Arthur Murray; dancer

1906 John Cameron Swayze; newsman

1913 Frances Langford; actress

1915 Muddy Waters (McKinley Morganfield); singer

1932 Richard G. Lugar; U.S. Senator

1942 Kitty Kelley; author

1946 Craig T. Nelson; actor

1948 Berry Oakley; musician, bassist

1950 Christine Lahti; actress

1952 Dave Hill; musician, guitarist

1965 Robert Downey, Jr.; actor

1966 Nancy McKeon; actress

1970 Barry Pepper; actor

1975 Scott Rolen; baseball

1979 Heath Ledger; actor

EVENTS FOR APRIL 4th

896 AD - Formosus ended his reign as pope.

1581 – Francis Drake was knighted for completing a circumnavigation of the world.

1687 - King James II ordered his *Declaration of Indulgence* read in church. The Indulgence was first issued for Scotland on 12 February, and then for England on 4 April 1687. It was a first step at establishing freedom of religion in the British Isles.

Playbill for Bryant's Mintrels, Mechanics' Hall, New York, 4 April 1859 (the night "Dixie" premiered). Public domain.

1818 – The United States Congress adopted the flag of the United States with 13 red and white stripes, and one star for each state (then 20).

1841 – William Henry Harrison died of pneumonia becoming the first President of the United States to die in office, and the one with the shortest term served to date (exactly one month).

1850 - The city of Los Angeles was incorporated. Its original name was El Pueblo de Nuestra Señora la Reina de los Ángeles del Río de Porciúncula (The Village of Our Lady, the Queen of the Angels of the river of Porziuncola).

1859 – In New York City, Bryant's Minstrels introduced "I Wish I was in Dixie's Land" (later named "Dixie") which became the Civil War song of the Confederacy.

1865 - It was reported that on this day President Lincoln awoke from a nightmare in which he had dreamed of his assassination. Ten days later, his dream came true.

1887 - Elected by the people of Argonia, Kansas, Susanna M. Salter became the United State's first woman mayor.

1905 - An earthquake in Kangra, India, killed 370,000 people.

1932 - After five years of research, Professor C.G. King, of the University of Pittsburgh, isolated Vitamin C.

1933 – The dirigible known as *The Akron* crashed in New Jersey, killing 73 people in one of the first air disasters in history. *The Akron* was the largest airship built in the United States when it took its first flight in August of 1931. In its short life of less than two years, it was involved in two fatal accidents.

USS *Akron* flying over the southern end of Manhattan, New York. Public domain.

1938 - After seven years singing on the radio, Kate Smith started a new noontime talk show called *Kate Smith's Column.*

1939 - Glenn Miller recorded "Moonlight Serenade" on RCA Bluebird records.

1945 – American troops liberated the Ohrdruf forced labor camp in Germany.

1945 – The Soviet Army took control of Hungary.

1949 - The North Atlantic Treaty Organization (NATO) treaty was signed.

1954 - Maestro Arturo Toscanini conducted his last concert with the NBC Symphony Orchestra at Carnegie Hall. During this concert Toscanini suffered a memory lapse reportedly caused by a transient ischemic attack (a "mini-stroke"), although some have attributed the lapse to having been secretly informed that NBC intended to end the broadcasts and disband the NBC orchestra. He never conducted live in public again.

1958 – Actress Lana Turner's boyfriend, Johnny Stompanato, was stabbed to death by her 14-year-old daughter, Cheryl.

1964 - The Beatles set a *Billboard* magazine Top 100 chart all-time record when the Fab Four claimed each of the top 5 songs.

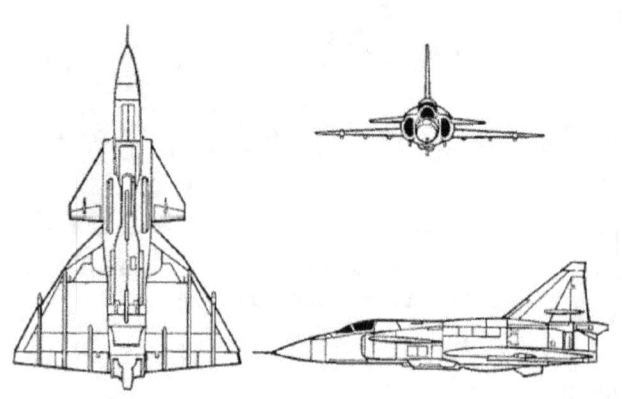

Drawing depicting the three axis views of the JA 37 Viggen. Public domain.

1965 – The Swedish Air Force revealed the first model of the new Saab Viggen fighter aircraft plane.

1967 – Martin Luther King, Jr. delivered his "Beyond Vietnam: A Time to Break Silence" speech in New York City's Riverside Church.

1968 - The Reverend Dr. Martin Luther King, Jr. was fatally shot in Memphis, Tennessee.

1968 - Bobby Goldsboro was awarded a gold record for the single, "Honey."

1969 - Dr. Denton Cooley implanted the first temporary artificial heart. Almost three days later a real heart became available for his patient. Dr. Cooley performed the transplant, and his patient died the following day.

1973 – The World Trade Center in New York City was officially dedicated.

1974 - Hank Aaron hit his 714th home run, tying Babe Ruth's record.

1975 – Microsoft was founded as a partnership between Bill Gates and Paul Allen in Albuquerque, New Mexico.

A rarely seen picture of the World Trade Center under construction. Photo taken by Pat Bianculli. Used by permission.

1984 - Bob Bell retired as Bozo the Clown on WGN-TV. The original Bozo was Larry Harmon.

1984 – President Ronald Reagan called for an international ban on chemical weapons.

1988 – Evan Mecham, Governor of Arizona, was convicted in his impeachment trial and removed from office. He was the first Arizona governor to be impeached.

1990 - Securities law violator Ivan Boesky was released from federal custody and served the remainder of his three-year term at a halfway house.

1991 – Senator John Heinz of Pennsylvania and six others were killed when a helicopter collided with their plane over an elementary school in Merion, Pennsylvania. The helicopter had been dispatched to check out a problem with the landing gear of Heinz's plane. While moving in for a closer look, the helicopter's rotor blades struck the bottom of the plane, causing both aircraft to lose control and crash. All aboard the two aircraft and two first-grade girls playing outside the school were killed.

1994 – Marc Andreessen and Jim Clark founded Netscape Communications Corporation under the name "Mosaic Communications Corporation."

The comet on the evening of its closest approach to Earth on March 25, 1996. Public domain.

1996 – Comet Hyakutake is imaged by the USA Asteroid Orbiter Near Earth Asteroid Rendezvous (a.k.a., NEAR – Shoemaker).

2002 – The Angolan government and UNITA rebels signed a peace treaty ending the Angolan Civil War.

2007 – Fifteen British Royal Navy personnel held in Iran were released by the Iranian President.

2008 – The raid on The Fundamentalist Church of Jesus Christ of Latter Day Saints owned ranch called the YFZ Ranch (also known as the Yearning for Zion Ranch) in Texas, resulted in 401 children being taken into protective custody, and 133 women taken into state custody.

APRIL 5th

BIRTHDAYS FOR APRIL 5th

1827 Joseph Lister; inventor

1856 Booker T. Washington; educator

1900 Spencer (Bonaventure) Tracy; actor

1901 Melvyn Douglas; actor

1908 Bette (Ruth Elizabeth) Davis; actress

1909 Albert R. Broccoli; American film producer

1916 Gregory Peck; actor

1920 Arthur Hailey; author

1926 Roger Corman; director

1928 Tony Williams; singer

1932 Billy Bland; American singer and songwriter

1934 Frank Gorshin; impressionist, actor

1934 Stanley Turrentine; jazz musician, saxophonist

1937 Colin Luther Powell; Chairman U.S. Joint Chiefs of Staff; Secretary of State

1940 Tommy Cash; songwriter

1941 Michael Moriarty; actor

1942 Peter Greenaway; director, writer

1943 Max Gail; American actor

1949 Dr. Judith A. Resnik; electrical engineer, astronaut

1950 Agnetha Faltskog; singer

1951 Rennie Stennett; baseball

1951 Brad Van Pelt; football

1952 Mitch Pileggi; actor

1966 Mike McCready; musician, guitarist

1981 Jorge de la Rosa; baseball

EVENTS FOR APRIL 5th

1355 - Charles IV was crowned in Rome as Holy Roman Emperor.

1614 - Pocahontas, daughter of King Powahatan, married the farmer John Rolfe in Jamestown, Virginia.

1722 - The Dutch explorer Jacob Roggeveen discovered Easter Island.

1792 – U.S. President George Washington exercised his authority to veto a bill; the first time this power was used in the United States.

1804 – The High Possil Meteorite, the first recorded meteorite in Scotland, fell in Possil.

1827 - James H. Hackett became the first actor from the United States to appear abroad, when he performed at Covent Garden in London, England.

1869 - Daniel Bakeman, the last surviving Revolutionary War soldier, died at the age of 109. (Incidentally, he was married to Susan Brewer Bakeman on August 29, 1772. She died aged 105 on Sept. 10, 1863. It was a marriage of 91 years, 12 days, the longest marriage on record to date.)

1892 - Walter H. Coe, of Providence, RI, received a patent for a "Method of Packing Decorative Films;" packaging decorative gold leaf in roll form. W.H. Coe Mfg. Co. manufactured the gold leaf in rolls 67 feet in length and in widths between 1/16 to 3-1/4 inches wide. The packaging method allowed precut widths to be matched to the application with correct lengths without need for overlapping pieces, thus waste was greatly reduced.

1923 - Akron, Ohio's Firestone Tire and Rubber Company began producing the first regular balloon tires.

1931 - Fox Film Corp. dropped John Wayne from its roster of actors. Wayne had played bit parts, but failed to impress the studio. In 1939, Wayne finally had his breakthrough in *Stagecoach*. Wayne went on to play in dozens of movies, including *True Grit* for which he won an Oscar in 1969.

Executive Order 6102 issued by Franklin D. Roosevelt in 1933 during the Great Depression requiring citizens to surrender their gold for which they were reimbursed. Public domain.

1933 – U.S. President Franklin D. Roosevelt signed Executive Order 6102 "forbidding the Hoarding of Gold Coin, Gold Bullion, and Gold Certificates" by U.S. citizens.

1942 - In New York City, the Ski Union of America was formed to become the Western hemisphere's governing body for amateur skiing.

1949 - *Fireside Theater* made its debut on NBC.

1949 - St. Anthony's hospital in Effingham, Illinois caught fire and burned to the ground, killing 70 people. As a result fire codes nationwide were improved. Due to extensive media coverage, including a *LIFE* magazine cover story, donations for rebuilding the hospital came from all 48 states and several foreign countries.

1951 – Julius and Ethel Rosenberg were sentenced to death for giving atomic secrets away to the Russians.

1955 - Richard J. Daley was elected mayor in the general election of Chicago, Illinois. Mayor Daley's service would

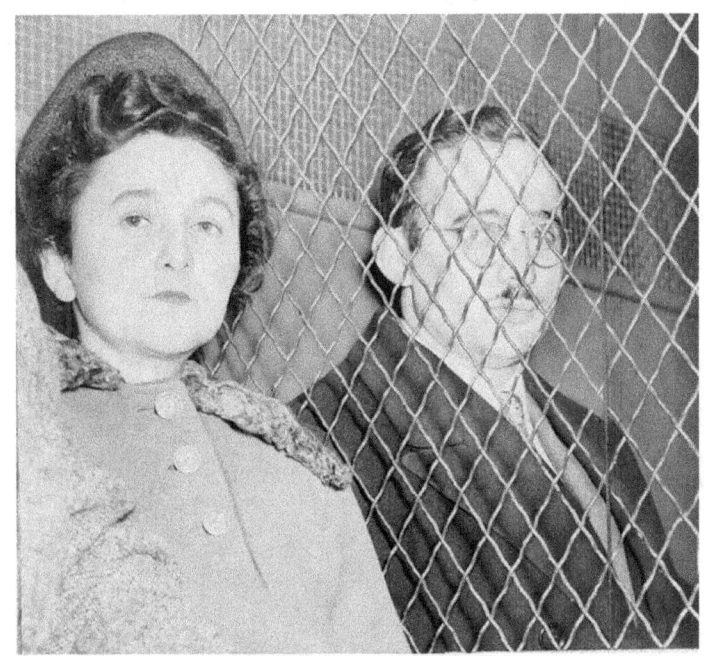

Julius and Ethel Rosenberg, separated by heavy wire screen as they leave U.S. Court House after being found guilty by jury. Public domain.

officially begin 10 days later.

1955 – Winston Churchill resigns as Prime Minister of the United Kingdom amid indications of failing health.

1976 - Billionaire playboy and filmmaker Howard Hughes died of kidney failure at the age of 70. Hughes was in extremely poor physical condition at the time of his death; X-rays revealed broken-off hypodermic needles still embedded in his arms and severe malnutrition.

1982 - After eight years of publication, *Record World* magazine ceased publishing and filed for bankruptcy protection.

1984 - Over 18,000 fans were in attendance to see the Utah Jazz play against the Los Angeles Lakers. During this game, Lakers' star Kareem Abdul-Jabbar scored the $31{,}420^{th}$ point of his career, breaking the NBA's all-time scoring record, which had been previously held by Wilt Chamberlain. By the way, the Lakers beat the Jazz 129 to 115.

1987 - The FOX Network began broadcasting with two Sunday night offerings: *Married . . . With Children* and *The Tracey Ullman Show*.

1988 - Arab gunmen seized a Kuwait Airways Boeing 747 carrying 115 passengers and killed two Kuwaitis. The hijacking lasted 16 days and ended with a Kuwaiti firefighter being killed along with another Kuwaiti military person.

1989 - The Polish government legalized the Solidarity Union, and introduced democratic measures into the political system.

1992 - Suada Dilberovic, a 23 year-old Croat medical student, along with Olga Sučić, became the first casualties of the War in Bosnia.

1994 - Kurt Cobain committed suicide inside his home in Seattle, Washington. His body was discovered three days later by Gary Smith, an electrician, who was installing a security system in the suburban house. Despite indications that Cobain, the lead singer of Nirvana, killed himself, several skeptics questioned the circumstances of his death and pinned responsibility on his wife, Courtney Love.

1998 – In Japan, the Akashi-Kaikyo Bridge linking Shikoku with Honshū and costing about $3.8 billion, opened to traffic, becoming the largest suspension bridge in the world.

The Akashi Bridge in Kobe in December 2005 Picture taken by Kim Rötzel. Used by permission.

1999 – Two Libyans suspected of bringing down Pan Am flight 103 in 1988 were handed over for eventual trial in the Netherlands.

2008 – Charlton Heston, known in his later years as the president of the National Rifle Association (NRA), died at the age of 84. Charlton Heston first earned a reputation in Hollywood for playing larger-than-life figures in epic movies such as *The Ten Commandments* and *Ben-Hur*.

2009 – North Korea launched its controversial Kwangmyongsong-2 rocket. The launch was officially announced to be a communications satellite on an Unha-2, however the US and South Korea claimed it was a test of a missile known in the west as Taepodong-2. The satellite passed over mainland Japan, which prompted an immediate reaction from the United Nations Security Council, as well as participating states of the Six-party talks.

APRIL 6th

BIRTHDAYS FOR APRIL 6th

1483 Raphael; painter,architect

1884 Walter Huston (Houghston); Academy Award-winning actor

1892 Lowell Thomas; American travel writer

1923 Herb Thomas; auto racer

1926 Gil Kane; cartoonist

1927 Gerry Mulligan; musician, composer

1928 James Watson; discoverer of structure of DNA

1929 Andre Previn; pianist, composer, conductor

1937 Merle Haggard; singer, songwriter

1937 Billy Dee Williams; actor

1942 Barry Levinson; Academy Award-winning director

1943 Marty (Martin William) Pattin; baseball

1945 Neal Boortz; American talk radio personality

1947 John Ratzenberger; actor

1952 Marilu Henner; actress

1953 Janet Lynn (Nowicki); ice skater

1969 Paul Rudd; actor

1970 Ari Meyers; actress

1970 Olaf Kolzig; hockey

1972 Jason Hervey; actor

1976 Candace Cameron; actress

EVENTS FOR APRIL 6th

648 BC - The earliest total solar eclipse, chronicled by Greeks, was recorded.

1199 - King Richard The Lionheart (Richard I) died after being wounded while besieging the castle of Chalus in France. His death was brought on by an infection following the removal of an arrow from his shoulder.

1580 – An earthquake badly damaged St Paul's Cathedral and other churches in London.

This is the building used as Federal Hall. It was actually the New York City Hall. Public domain.

1789 – The first United States Congress began regular sessions at Federal Hall in New York City.

1860 – The Reorganized Church of Jesus Christ of Latter Day Saints (later renamed "Community of Christ") was organized by Joseph Smith III and others at Amboy, Illinois

1862 – The Battle of Shiloh began in Tennessee. There forces under Union General Ulysses S. Grant met Confederate troops led by General Albert Sidney Johnston.

1865 – During the Battle of Sayler's Creek, Confederate General Robert E. Lee's Army of Northern Virginia fought its last major battle while in retreat from Richmond, Virginia.

1886 – The city of Vancouver, British Columbia, was incorporated. Two months after its incorporation, the city was virtually wiped out by a fire. The city quickly rebuilt.

1888 – Thomas Green Clemson died and left his estate to the State of South Carolina to establish Clemson Agricultural College.

1893 – Salt Lake Temple of The Church of Jesus Christ of Latter-day Saints was dedicated by Wilford Woodruff, the 4th President of The Church of Jesus Christ of Latter-day Saints.

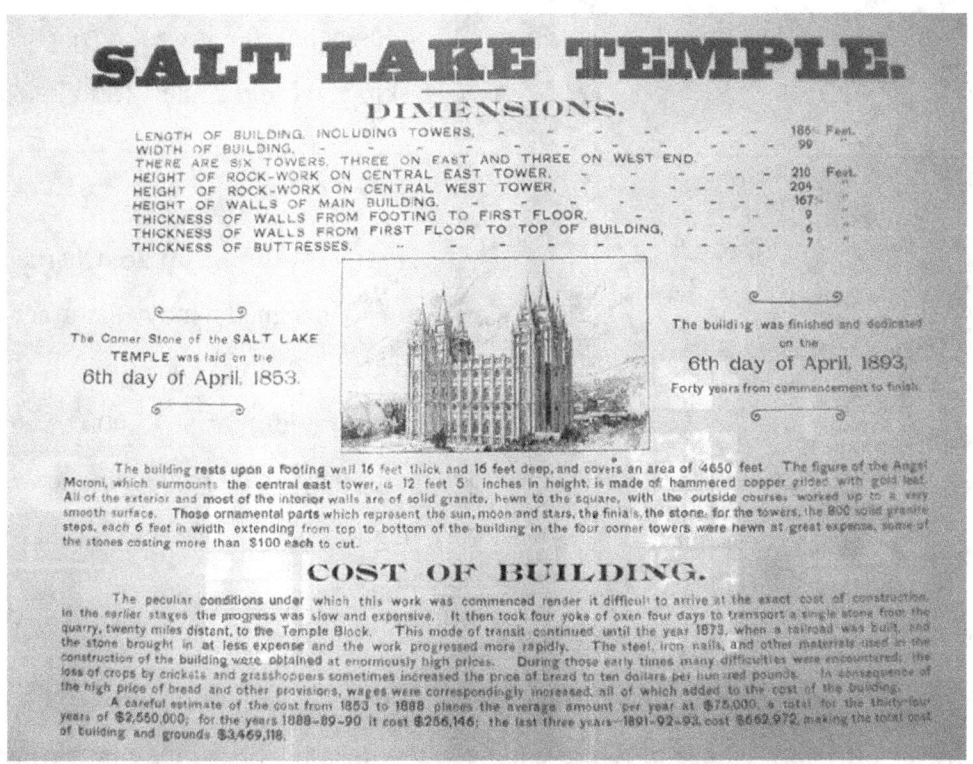

Details of Salt Lake City Temple construction. Used by permission.

1893 - The longest boxing match to date was held between Andy Bowen and Jack Burke in New Orleans. The fight lasted 111 rounds. It took 7 hours and 19 minutes until referee John Duffy called "no contest" after both men were too dazed and tired to come out of their corners.

1895 - Writer Oscar Wilde was arrested for being a homosexual and sentenced to two years of hard labor.

James B. Connolly, the first Olympic Champion since the 4th century AD. Public domain.

1896 – In Athens, Greece, the first modern Olympic Games began 1,500 years after the original games were banned by Roman Emperor Theodosius I. The very first event was won by James B. Connolly of Boston, Massachusetts; it was the hop, skip and jump contest (also know as "the triple jump").

1916 - At the age of 26, Charlie Chaplin signed a movie contract with the Mutual Film Corporation, for $675,000 a year. This agreement made him the highest paid movie actor at the time.

1917 - Two days after the U.S. Senate voted 82-6 to declare war against Germany, the U.S. House of Representatives endorsed the declaration by a vote of 373-50, and America formally entered World War I.

1925 - Eddie Cantor recorded, "If You Knew Susie."

1926 – Varney Airlines made its first commercial flight as an air-mail carrier. Varney would later merge with three other companies to form United Airlines.

1927 - When the Department of Commerce began issuing aviator's license, William P. MacCracken, Jr. earned license #1.

1929 – The Louisiana House of Representatives attempted, but failed, to impeach Governor Huey P. Long.

1947 – The first *Tony Awards* were presented for theatrical achievements.

1950 - A train dropped from a bridge in Tangua, Brazil, killing 110 people. Twenty-two cars made up the Leopoldina Railways train that departed Rio de Janeiro for Victoria, Espirito Santo. The passenger cars were filled with people vacationing over the Easter holidays. The train left after midnight and had gone almost 60 miles when it approached the bridge over the Indios River at about 1:30 a.m. The river, swollen from days of torrential rains in the area, had undermined the bridge's foundation. As it was about halfway across, the locomotive and five cars (two carrying only baggage) plunged into the river. The remaining 17 cars managed to stay on the tracks despite the connected cars being dragged into the river.

1956 – Capitol Tower, home of Capitol Records in Hollywood, California, was dedicated, making it the first circular office tower designed in the United States.

1956 - Paramount Pictures signed Elvis Presley to a seven-year contract, only five days after he made his first screen test in Hollywood.

1958 - Arnold Palmer won his first major, professional golf tournament by taking the Masters by one stroke in Augusta, Georgia.

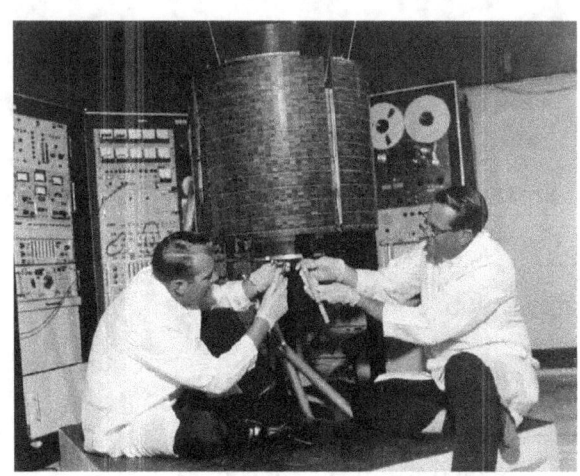

Engineers Stanley R. Peterson (left) and Ray Bowerman (right), checkout the Early Bird, the world's first communication satellite. Public domain.

1965 – Early Bird I, the world's first commercial communications satellite, was launched from Cape Kennedy, Florida. It became operational on June 28.

1968 – In Richmond, Indiana's downtown district, a double explosion killed 41 and injured 150. The primary explosion was due to natural gas leaking from one or more faulty transmission lines under the Marting Arms sporting goods store at 6th and Main Street. A secondary explosion was caused by gunpowder stored inside the building.

1968 – Stanley's Kubrick's science-fiction classic *2001: A Space Odyssey* made its debut in movie theaters.

1968 - Pierre Trudeau became the Liberal Party's prime minister of Canada, succeeding Lester Pearson.

The centrifuge set used for filming scenes depicting interior of the spaceship Discovery in *2001: A Space Odyssey*. Used by permission.

1973 - The Stylistics received a gold

record for, "Break Up to Make Up."

1974 - The first concert film featuring a soundtrack in quadraphonic sound (the forerunner of surround sound) opened. *Ladies and Gentlemen: The Rolling Stones* was a hit.

1992 - *Barney and Friends* premiered on PBS.

1998 – Travelers Group announced an agreement to undertake the $76 billion merger between Travelers and Citicorp, and the merger was completed on October 8, of that year, forming Citibank.

1998 - Country singer Tammy Wynette died at age 55.

2004 – Rolandas Paksas became the first president of Lithuania to be peacefully removed from office by impeachment.

2005 – Kurdish leader Jalal Talabani became Iraqi president; Shiite Arab Ibrahim al-Jaafari was named premier the next day.

2009 – A 6.3 magnitude earthquake occurred near L'Aquila, Italy, killing at least 253.

APRIL 7th

BIRTHDAYS FOR APRIL 7th

1770 William Wordsworth; poet

1786 William King; 13th U.S. Vice President

1860 Will Keith Kellogg; American cereal manufacturer

1869 David Fairchild; botanist, government official, explorer

1897 Walter Winchell; vaudeville, journalist, gossip columnist

1908 Percy Faith; Grammy Award-winning orchestra leader, composer

1915 Billie Holiday (Eleanora Fagan); singer

1928 James Garner (Baumgarner); actor

1933 Wayne Rogers; actor

1935 Bobby Bare; Grammy Award-winning singer

1935 Hodding Carter III; journalist

1937 Gail Cogdill; football

1938 Jerry Brown; California Governor

1939 Francis Ford Coppola; Academy Award-winning director

1939 David Frost; TV host

1943 Mick Abrahams; musician, guitarist

1943 Spencer Dryden; musician, drummer

1944 Gerhard Schröder; Chancellor of Germany

1947 Patricia Bennett; singer

1949 John Oates; songwriter, singer

1951 Janis Ian (Fink); Grammy Award-winning singer, songwriter

1952 Bruce Gary; musician, drummer

1954 Tony Dorsett; Football Hall Famer

1954 Jackie Chan; actor

1960 Buster (James) Douglas; boxing

1964 Russell Crowe; actor

EVENTS FOR APRIL 7th

A page from the original manuscript of the Book of Mormon, covering 1 Nephi 4:38- 5:14. Public domain.

1118 - Pope Gelasius II excommunicated Henry V, Holy Roman Emperor, at Capua.

1348 – Charles University was founded in Prague.

1795 – France adopted the "meter" as the basic measure of length.

1823 - French forces under Louis de Bourbon invaded Spain, beginning the Franco-Spanish war.

1827 - John Walker, an English chemist, sells the first "friction match." He had invented it the previous year.

1829 – Joseph Smith, Jr., founder of The Church of Jesus Christ of Latter-day Saints, began translating the Book of Mormon, with Oliver Cowdery as his scribe.

1906 – Mount Vesuvius erupted and devastated Naples, Italy.

1925 - Adolph Hitler formally renounced his Austrian citizenship. For the next seven years, Adolph did not claim citizenship to any country and risked deportation from Germany.

1927 - The first simultaneous telecast of image and sound took place when Secretary of Commerce Herbert Hoover read a speech in Washington, D.C. It was transmitted to Bell Telephone Laboratories in New York City, where an audience saw and heard a tiny televised image of Hoover, less than 3 inches square.

1940 – Booker T. Washington becomes the first African American to be depicted on a United States postage stamp.

1943 – Germans ordered 1,100 Jews to undress to their underwear and march through the city of Terebovlia, Ukraine to the nearby village of Plebanivka where they were shot dead and buried in ditches.

The Booker T. Washington stamp. Public domain.

1943 - Adolf Hitler and Benito Mussolini met for an Axis conference in Salzburg.

1945 – The Japanese battleship *Yamato*, the largest battleship ever constructed, was sunk by American planes 200 miles north of Okinawa while en-route to a suicide mission in Operation Ten-Go.

1948 - The constitution of the World Health Organization (WHO) went into force.

1956 - A declaration signed by Morocco and Spain recognized the independence of Morocco.

1963 - The Socialist Federal Republic of Yugoslavia was established with Marshall Tito as its president for life.

1964 – IBM announced the System/360, an IBM mainframe computer system that could store a whopping 256 kB of main storage.

NASA took this image of the System/360 Model 91 sometime in the late 60s. Public domain.

1970 - Today John Wayne, a veteran of over 200 films, won his first and only Oscar, when he secured the "Best Actor In A Leading Role" award for *True Grit*.

1970 – A Grand Jury closed the investigation of Sen. Ted Kennedy over the car crash in which Mary Jo Kopechne died at Chappaquiddick in 1969.

1973 - Vicki Lawrence had a #1 single with "The Night the Lights Went Out in Georgia."

1978 – The development of the neutron bomb was canceled by President Jimmy Carter.

1980 – Through Executive Order 12205, President Jimmy Carter broke off diplomatic relations with Iran because of the detention of United States embassy hostages in Tehran.

1983 – Astronauts Story Musgrave and Don Peterson performed the first space shuttle spacewalk.

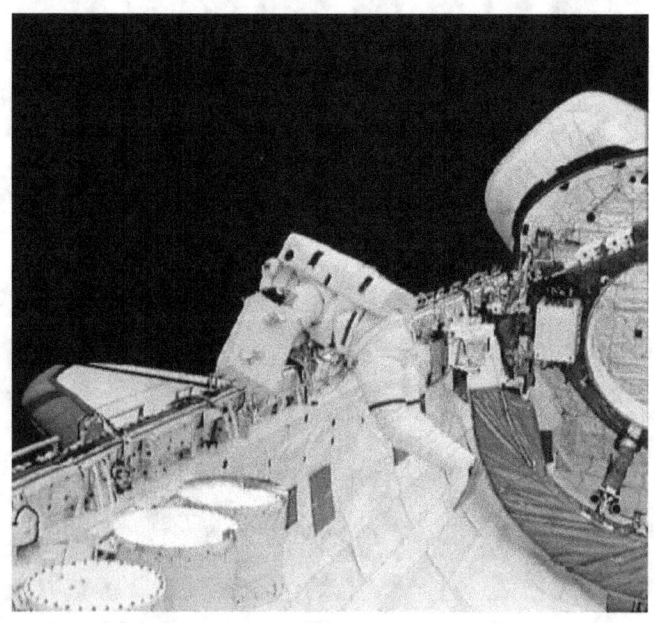

Using an Extravehicular Mobility Unit, Story Musgrave works untethered aboard the Space Shuttle Challenger. Public domain.

1990 - *The Scandinavian Star*, a Bahamas-registered car and passenger ferry operated by the Da No Line, caught fire while on a journey; 158 people were killed.

1990 – John Poindexter was found guilty of five charges for his part in the Iran-Contra Affair (the conviction was later reversed on appeal).

1994 – Auburn Calloway attempted to hijack FedEx Flight 705 and crash it to enrich his family with his life insurance policy. The crew subdued him and landed the aircraft safely.

1998 - British-born pop star George Michael was arrested on suspicion of committing a lewd act in a public park restroom.

2001 – NASA launched the Mars Odyssey.

An artist's impression of the Mars Odyssey in Martian orbit. Public domain.

2003 – U.S. troops captured Baghdad; Saddam Hussein's regime fell two days later.

2009 – Former Peruvian President Alberto Fujimori was sentenced to 25 years in prison for ordering killings and kidnappings by security forces.

APRIL 8th

BIRTHDAYS FOR APRIL 8th

1842 Elizabeth Bacon Custer; wife of George Armstrong Custer

1892 Mary Pickford (Gladys Louise Smith); Academy Award-winning actress

1912 Sonja Henie; ice skater; Olympic gold medalist

1918 Betty Ford; U.S. First Lady

1920 Carmen McRae; singer

1923 Edward Mulhare; actor

1926 Shecky Greene (Fred Sheldon Greenfield); comedian

1938 Kofi Annan; UN Secretary General

1941 Peggy Lennon; singer

1943 John (Frederick) Hiller; baseball

1944 Roger Chapman; singer

1946 Jim (James Augustus) "Catfish" Hunter; baseball

1946 Stuart Pankin; actor

1947 Steve Howe; musician, guitarist, singer

1954 Gary Carter; sportscaster

1960 John Schneider; American actor

1961 Mark Gregory Clayton; football

1961 Richard Hatch; winner of Survivor TV program

1962 Izzy Stradlin; American musician

1963 Julian Lennon; singer

1963 Terry Porter; basketball

1964 Biz Markie; American rapper/disc jockey

1966 Robin Wright Penn; actress

1968 Patricia Arquette; actress

1984 Taran Noah Smith; actor

EVENTS FOR APRIL 8*th*

1513 - Florida was discovered and claimed for Spain by Juan Ponce de León.

1730 – Shearith Israel, the first synagogue in New York City, was dedicated.

So-called "Venus de Milo" (Aphrodite from Melos). Parian marble, ca. 130-100 BC? Found in Melos in 1820. Public domain.

1820 – The Venus de Milo was discovered on the Aegean island of Melos.

1834 - Cornelius Lawrence, eventual mayor of New York City, became the first United States mayor elected by popular vote in a city election.

1873 - Alfred Paraf of New York City received patent #137,564 for the "improvement in purifying and separating fats." This product is known better today as oleomargarine.

1893 – The first recorded college basketball game was played in Beaver Falls, Pennsylvania. (Incidentally,

Geneva College defeated the New Brighton YMCA. The final score could not be confirmed.)

1895 – The Supreme Court of the United States ruled in *Pollock v. Farmers' Loan & Trust Company* unapportioned income tax to be unconstitutional.

1898 - Lord Kitchener captured the Mahdi at Atbara River after defeating his Sudanese army.

1904 – Longacre Square in Midtown Manhattan was renamed "Times Square" after The *New York Times*.

The site of One Times Square, north side of 42nd Street, Broadway to 7th Avenue, circa 1880. Public domain.

1906 – Auguste Deter, the first person to be diagnosed with Alzheimer's disease, died at age 56.

1913 – The 17th Amendment to the United States Constitution, requiring direct election of Senators, became law.

1935 - The United States Congress approved the Works Progress Administration (WPA - later called the Work Projects Administration).

1941 - Earle Graser, voice of radio's *The Lone Ranger* for eight years, died in an auto accident.

1943 – U.S. President Franklin D. Roosevelt, in an attempt to check inflation, froze wages and prices, prohibited workers from changing jobs unless the war effort would be aided thereby, and barred rate increases by common carriers and public utilities.

1946 - The League of Nations began its final session in Geneva after being replaced by the United Nations.

1947 - The Allstate Insurance Company issued the first illustrated insurance policy.

1952 – U.S. President Harry Truman called for the seizure of all domestic steel mills to prevent a nationwide strike.

1963 - The movie *Lawrence of Arabia* won seven Academy Awards, including "Best Picture."

1968 - The Beatles went gold with the single, "Lady Madonna."

1974 – It was a historic night in sports at Atlanta, Georgia's Fulton County Stadium. Hank Aaron broke Babe Ruth's home run record.

1975 - *The Godfather Part II* became the first movie sequel to win the "Best

The site where Atlanta-Fulton County Stadium once stood is now a parking lot for Turner Field. The fence and wall display in the center of the picture commemorates the spot at which Hank Aaron's 715th home run landed on April 8, 1974. Public domain.

Picture" award (the original, *The Godfather*, won the 1972 Oscar for "Best Picture").

1986 - Clint Eastwood won a landslide victory on this date to become Mayor of Carmel-by-the-Sea, a California resort town of 4,700 people. He spent more than $40,000 to campaign for the $200 a week position and served only one term.

1986 - Jennifer Guinness (of the well-known brewing family) was released after having been kidnapped in Ireland for a 2 million-pound ransom.

1990 - Ryan White, the Indiana youth who contracted AIDS through a blood transfusion, died on this date in Indianapolis at age 18.

1992 - Arthur Ashe, former Wimbledon champion, announced in a reluctant press conference that he had AIDS which he had contracted from blood transfusions during one of his two heart surgeries.

1992 - After genetic fingerprinting tests, German and Israeli authorities said they were certain that Josef Mengele died in Brazil in 1979.

1994 - South Africa's four key political leaders met at a bush camp in lion country for a peace summit aimed at stopping violence threatening free and fair elections.

2000 – Nineteen Marines were killed when a V-22 Osprey tilt-rotor aircraft crashed near Marana, Arizona.

2004 – The Humanitarian Ceasefire Agreement is signed by the Sudanese government and two rebel groups.

2004 – U.S. National Security Advisor, Condoleezza Rice, testified before the 9/11 Commission becoming the first sitting National Security Advisor to testify on matters of policy.

2005 - Eric Rudolph agreed to plead guilty to a series of bombings, including the fatal bombing at the 1996 Olympics in Atlanta, in order to avoid the death penalty

The three wind turbines at the centre of the Bahrain World Trade Center. Photo by Tim Miller. Used by permission.

2006 – The bodies of eight men, all shot to death, were found in a field in Ontario, Canada. The murders were soon linked to the "Bandidos" motorcycle gang.

2008 – The construction of the world's first building to integrate wind turbines was completed in Bahrain.

APRIL 9th

BIRTHDAYS FOR APRIL 9th

1883 Frank King; cartoonist

1889 Efrem Zimbalist, Sr.; Russian violinist

1903 Ward Bond; actor

1926 Hugh Hefner; publisher

1928 Tom Lehrer; songwriter

1932 Jim Fowler; American zoologist

1932 Carl Perkins; singer

1932 Paul Krassner; editor, journalist

1933 Jean-Paul Belmondo; actor

1935 Avery Schreiber; comedian

1937 Marty Krofft; Canadian television producer

1939 Michael Learned; Emmy Award-winning actress

1940 Jim Roberts; hockey

1942 Brandon de Wilde; actor

1943 Terry Knight; singer

1945 Alden Roche; football

1946 Nate Colbert; baseball

1946 Les Gray; singer

1948 Michel Parizeau; hockey

1954 Dennis Quaid; actor

1957 Steve Ballesteros; golf

1961 Mark Kelly; musician, keyboardist

1966 Cynthia Nixon; actress

1971 Jacques Villeneueve; Indianapolis 500 winner

1974 Jenna Jameson; American pornographic actress

1979 Albert Hammond, Jr.; American guitarist

1979 Keshia Knight Pulliam; actress

EVENTS FOR APRIL 9th

1667 - The first public art exhibition was held at the Palais-Royale in Paris.

1682 – Robert Cavelier de La Salle discovered the mouth of the Mississippi River, claimed it for France and named it Louisiana.

1833 - The first municipally supported public library opened in Peterborough, New Hampshire.

1859 - Samuel Clemens (Mark Twain) became a licensed riverboat pilot on the Mississippi River; this was before he became a serious writer.

1865 - The United States civil war ended when Confederate General Robert E. Lee surrendered to Union General Ulysses S. Grant at Appomattox.

1866 - The Civil Rights Act of 1866 passed over President Andrew Johnson's veto.

1867 –Passing by a single vote, the United States Senate ratified a treaty with Russia for the purchase of Alaska.

1870 – Believing that its work had been completed, the American Anti-Slavery Society dissolved.

1881 - Billy the Kid was found guilty of murdering the Lincoln County, New Mexico, sheriff and was sentenced to hang.

1913 – Four days after the opening game, the Brooklyn Dodgers' Ebbets Field formally opened to the public.

Miss Genevieve Ebbets, youngest daughter of Charley Ebbets, throwing the first ball at opening of Ebbets Field. Circa April 5, 1913. Public domain.

1928 - Actress Mae West made her New York debut in a titillating play called *Diamond Lil*.

1940 - Germany invaded Norway and Denmark during World War II.

1941 - The PGA established the Golf Hall of Fame.

1942 – During World War II United States forces surrendered on the Bataan Peninsula. The Japanese Navy launched an air raid on Trincomalee in Ceylon (Sri Lanka); Royal Navy aircraft carrier HMS *Hermes* and Royal Australian Navy Destroyer HMAS *Vampire* were sunk off the island's east coast.

1945 - National Football League officials decreed it mandatory that football players wear socks in all league games.

1947 - Tornadoes struck west Texas and Oklahoma, killing 169 and injuring 970.

1950 - Bob Hope made his first network television debut on NBC-TV's *Star-Spangled Review.*

1957 - The Suez Canal was cleared for all shipping.

1959 – NASA introduced America's first astronauts to the press: Scott Carpenter, L. Gordon Cooper Jr., John H. Glenn Jr., Virgil "Gus" Grissom, Walter Schirra Jr., Alan Shepard Jr., and Donald Slayton.

1963 - Winston Churchill became the first (and to date the only) honorary United States citizen.

Back Row - Shepard, Grissom, Cooper; Front Row - Schirra, Slayton, Glenn, Carpenter. This was the only time the seven astronauts would appear together in pressure suits. Slayton and Glenn were wearing spray-painted work boots.

1965 - *TIME Magazine's* cover featured the entire "Peanuts" gang.

1965 – Major league baseball had its first indoor game. President Lyndon B. Johnson attended the opening of the Astrodome in Houston, Texas.

1967 - The first Boeing 737 rolled out for its maiden flight.

1968 - Martin Luther King Jr. was buried.

1969 – The "Chicago Eight" pleaded not guilty to federal charges of conspiracy to incite a riot at the 1968 Democratic National Convention in Chicago, Illinois.

1969 – The supersonic aircraft *Concorde* made its maiden flight, from Bristol to Fairford in England.

Cockpit of the *Concorde*. Photo by Christian Kath. Used by permission.

1970 - Paul McCartney announced that he would leave the Beatles.

1975 – The first game was held of the Philippine Basketball Association, at the time the second oldest professional basketball league in the world.

1977 - The Swedish pop group Abba celebrated their first American #1 hit. "Dancing Queen."

1980 – The Iraqi regime of Saddam Hussein killed philosopher Muhammad Baqir al-Sadr and his sister Bint al-Huda after three days of torture.

1983 - The 6th space shuttle mission, *Challenger* 1, returned to Earth. This was the *Challenger's* 1st mission.

1991 - Georgia voted to secede from the Soviet Union.

1992 - John Major was elected prime minister of England.

1992 – A U.S. Federal Court found former Panamanian dictator Manuel Noriega guilty of drug and racketeering charges. He was sentenced to 30 years in prison.

1999 - *Never Been Kissed*, starring Drew Barrymore as a copy editor who goes undercover at a high school to report on teenagers, opened in United States theaters.

The April 2003 toppling of Saddam Hussein's statue in Firdos Square in Baghdad shortly after the capture of the city.

2002 – The funeral of Queen Elizabeth (Elizabeth Angela Marguerite Bowes-Lyon) was held at Westminster Abbey.

2003 – Baghdad fell to American forces; the statue of Saddam Hussein statue was toppled as Iraqis turned on symbols of their former leader.

2005 – Tens of thousands of demonstrators, many of them supporters of Shia cleric Moqtada al-Sadr, marched through Baghdad and denounced the U.S. occupation of Iraq, 2 years after the fall of Saddam Hussein, and rallied in the square where his statue fell in 2003.

2005 – Charles, Prince of Wales, married Camilla Parker Bowles in a civil ceremony.

APRIL 10th

BIRTHDAYS FOR APRIL 10th

1735 Button Gwinnett; Signer of the US Declaration of Independence

1796 James Bowie; American pioneer and soldier

1829 William Booth; Salvation Army founder, author

1847 Joseph Pulitzer; publisher

1880 Frances Perkins; Secretary of Labor

1885 Bernard Gimbel; merchant

1911 Martin Denny; composer, arranger, pianist

1915 Harry Morgan (Bratsberg); Emmy Award-winning actor

1921 Chuck Connors (Kevin Joseph Aloysius Connors); actor

1921 Sheb Wooley; comic, singer, songwriter

1926 Junior Samples; American southern comedian

1929 Max Von Sydow; actor

1932 Omar Sharif (Michael Shalhoub); actor

1934 David Halberstam; author

1936 John Madden; football

1936 Bobbie Smith; singer

1938 Dandy Don Meredith; football

1941 Paul Edward Theroux; author

1947 Bunny Wailer (Neville O'Riley); musician, percussionist, singer, songwriter

1950 Ken Griffey Sr.; baseball

1952 Steven Seagal; actor

1954 Peter MacNicol; actor

1960 Brian Setzer; musician, guitarist, singer

1968 Orlando Jones; American actor and comedian

1988 Haley Joel Osment; actor

EVENTS FOR APRIL 10th

1816 – The United States Government approved the creation of the Second Bank of the United States.

1834 – A fire at the Lalaurie House, a mansion in New Orleans, Louisiana, led to the discovery of a torture chamber where slaves were routinely brutalized by Delphine Lalaurie. Rescuers found a 70 year-old black woman trapped in the kitchen during the fire because she was chained up while Lalaurie was

The LaLaurie Mansion. From a postcard circa 1906. Public domain.

saving her furniture. The woman later revealed that she had set the fire in an attempt to escape Lalaurie's torture. She led authorities up to the attic where seven slaves were discovered tied with spiked iron collars.

The original patent drawings for Walter Hunt's safety pin. Public domain.

1849 – New York City's Walter Hunt patented the safety pin. He thought his invention would only be a temporary convenience and sold the patent for $400.

1864 - Archduke Maximilian of Austria accepted the throne of Mexico.

1866 – The American Society for the Prevention of Cruelty to Animals (ASPCA) was founded in New York City by Henry Bergh.

1906 - O. Henry's second short story collection, *The Four Million*, was published. The collection includes one of his most beloved stories, "The Gift of the Magi," about a poor but devoted couple who each sacrifice their most valuable possession to buy a gift for the other.

RMS *Titanic* departing Southampton, for the first and only time, on 10 April 1912. Public domain.

1912 – The RMS *Titanic* left port in Southampton, England for her first and only voyage.

1916 – The Professional Golfers Association of America (PGA) was created in New York City.

1922 - The Genoa Conference opened to discuss the reconstruction of Europe after World War I.

1925 – *The Great Gatsby* by F. Scott Fitzgerald was first published in New York City, by Charles Scribner's Sons.

1932 - Paul von Hindenburg received 18,661,736 votes in the German presidential elections, defeating Adolf Hitler's 11,328,571 votes.

1939 - *Dr. I.Q., the Mental Banker* debuted. The traveling show broadcast live from different cities across the country. Dr. I.Q., the quizmaster, interrogated contestants at a rate faster than one question a minute. Contestants were selected from the audience and awarded a varying number of silver dollars for correct answers. Proud winners would also occasionally receive a box of candy bars from the show's sponsor. The show ran until 1950.

1953 - *House of Wax*, starring Vincent Price, the first Warner Brothers 3-D film, premiered in New York City.

1961 - Gary Player from South Africa became the first foreign golfer to win the Masters Golf Tournament in Augusta, Georgia.

1962 - Stuart Sutcliffe, the original bass player for The Beatles, died of a brain hemorrhage. Sutcliffe and John Lennon are credited with coming up with the name for the Beatles.

1963 – The United States submarine USS *Thresher*, an atomic submarine, sank in the Atlantic off Cape Cod, Massachusetts with the loss of 129 lives.

1971 – In an attempt to thaw relations with the United States, the People's Republic of China hosted the U.S. table tennis team for a weeklong visit. This event became known as "Ping Pong Diplomacy."

1972 – "Theme from Shaft" received an Academy Award for Best Original Song in a film in 1971.

1972 - The U.S. and the Soviet Union joined some 70 nations in signing "The Biological Weapons Convention," an agreement to ban biological warfare.

1973 – One hundred-four people died when a plane crashed in Switzerland while attempting to land at Basel.

1978 - Volkswagen became the second (after Rolls-Royce) non-American automobile manufacturer to open a plant in the United States, commencing production of the Rabbit, the North American version of the Volkswagen Golf, in New Stanton, Pennsylvania with a unionized (UAW) workforce (the plant closed in 1992).

1979 - A tornado hit Wichita Falls, Texas, killing 42 people (the most notable of 26 tornadoes that day).

The World-famous "Rock of Gilbralter," taken from the west side. Public domain.

1980 – Spain and the United Kingdom agree to reopen the border between Gibraltar and Spain; it had been closed since 1969.

1986 – Sixty-five million shares of Navistar International stock changed hands in a single-block trade, the largest transaction to date executed on the NYSE.

1988 - The Great Seto Bridge opened to traffic in Japan.

1991 – A rare tropical storm developed in the South Atlantic Ocean near Angola; the first to be documented by satellites.

1992 - Comedian Sam Kinison was killed in an auto accident outside of Needles, California. He was buried in Memorial Park Cemetery in Tulsa, Oklahoma.

1993 - South African Communist Party leader Chris Hani was assassinated.

2005 - Tiger Woods won his 4th Masters Golf Tournament at Augusta National Golf Club after a 15-foot birdie on the first hole of the sudden-death playoff against Chris DiMarco.

APRIL 11th

BIRTHDAYS FOR APRIL 11th

1755 James Parkinson; English physician

1794 Edward Everett; 15th Governor of Massachusetts

1862 Charles Evans Hughes; 11th Chief Justice of the US Supreme Court

1864 Lillie P. Bliss; co-founder of New York City's Museum of Modern Art

1899 Percy Julian; scientist

1907 Paul Douglas; actor

1908 Jane Bolin; attorney, judge

1913 Oleg Cassini; fashion designer

1921 Dorothy Shay (Sims); singer

1928 Ethel Kennedy; widow of U.S. Attorney General Robert Kennedy

1931 Johnny Sheffield; actor

1932 Joel Grey (Katz); Academy award-winning actor

1933 Tony Brown; journalist

1939 Louise Lasser; actress

1941 Ellen Goodman; Pulitzer prize winning columnist

1943 Harley Race; American professional wrestler

1944 Joe Beauchamp; football

1947 Peter Riegert; actor

1947 Meshach Taylor; actor

1950 Bill Irwin; actor, choreographer

1951 Sid Monge; baseball

1956 Neville Staples; singer

1958 Stuart Adamson; musician, guitarist, singer

1964 Bret Saberhagen; baseball

1966 Lisa Stansfield; singer, songwriter

1969 Dustin Rhodes; American professional wrestler

1970 Delroy Pearson; singer

EVENTS FOR APRIL 11th

1775- The last execution for witchcraft in Germany took place.

1814 – The Treaty of Fontainebleau ended the War of the Sixth Coalition against Napoleon Bonaparte, and forced him to abdicate unconditionally for the first time.

1862 – Rebels surrender Ft. Pulaski during the U.S. Civil War.

1865 – President Abraham Lincoln made his last public speech. During this speech Lincoln gave support for the idea of voting rights for blacks. In the audience was a man named John Wilkes

Wall of Fort Pulaski National Monument damaged by artillery shelling. Public domain.

Booth who was later quoted as saying, "That is the last speech he will ever give." Booth made good on his threat three nights later.

1876 - The Benevolent and Protective Order of Elks (BPOE; also known as the Elks Lodge) was organized. Originally, the name of the organization was the Jolly Corks Club.

1898 - United States President William McKinley asked for the Spanish-American War declaration.

Movie poster for *The Tramp*. Public domain.

1905 – Albert Einstein revealed his Theory of Relativity (special relativity).

1915 – *The Tramp*, Charlie Chaplin's third film and first comic masterpiece, was released.

1921 - Iowa imposed the first state cigarette tax.

1921 - The world's first sports broadcast was aired on station KDKA by Florent Gibson of the Pittsburg Star newspaper. The commentary Florent delivered was of a fight between Johnny Ray and Johnny Dundee.

1945 - United States soldiers liberated the Nazi concentration camp Buchenwald.

1951 –United States President Harry Truman fired Gen. Douglas McArthur.

DECLASSIFIED
E.O. 11652, Sec. 3(E) and 5(D)
[illegible handwriting]
By [illegible], NARS Date 2-7-75

PROPOSED ORDER TO GENERAL MacARTHUR TO BE SIGNED BY
THE PRESIDENT

      I deeply regret that it becomes my duty as President and Commander in Chief of the United States military forces to replace you as Supreme Commander, Allied Powers; Commander in Chief, United Nations Command; Commander in Chief, Far East; and Commanding General, U. S. Army, Far East.

      You will turn over your commands, effective at once, to Lt. Gen. Matthew B. Ridgway. You are authorized to have issued such orders as are necessary to complete desired travel to such place as you select.

      My reasons for your replacement, ~~which~~ will be made public concurrently with the delivery to you of the foregoing order, ~~will be communicated to you by Secretary Pace.~~ *and are contained in the next following message.*

Harry Truman

The actual proposed message to Gen. MacArthur. Image courtesy of the Harry S. Truman Library and Museum. Public domain.

1954 – According to "True Knowledge, the Internet Answer Engine," this was the most boring day since 1900.

1956 - Elvis Presley reached #1 with his first double-sided hit, featuring "Heartbreak Hotel" and "I Was the One."

1961 – At the tender age of 19 Bob Dylan made his New York City stage debut at Gerde's "Folk City," a small Greenwich Village club.   For two weeks, Bob served as the opening act for John Lee Hooker.

1962 - The New York Mets played their first regular season game. They lost to the Cardinals 11-4.

1965 – Fifty-one tornadoes hit in six Midwestern states, killing 256 people during the Palm Sunday tornado outbreak.

1965 - Jack Nicklaus won the Masters golf title for the second time.

1968 - Rescue workers picked up the last survivors of the *Wahine* ferry accident. The ferry capsized after hitting sharp rocks off the coast of Wellington, New Zealand, the previous day. Fifty-one of the more than 800 passengers and crew on board perished in the accident.

1968 - United States President Lyndon B Johnson signed the Civil Rights Act of 1968.

1970 - Apollo 13 was launched to the moon; unable to land, it returned in 6 days.

1976 – The Apple I computer was created. When it went on sale in July of the same year, its price tag was $666.66.

1979 - Ugandan dictator Idi Amin was overthrown.

1981 - Guitarist Eddie Van Halen and actress Valerie Bertinelli (of CBS-TV's "One Day at a Time") were married in Los Angeles, California. Their marriage lasted more than 24 years.

1986 – The FBI Miami shootout erupted between eight Federal Bureau of Investigation agents and two heavily armed and well-trained gunmen. Four people were left dead and five more were injured.

1986 - Halley's Comet made its closest approach to Earth. If you missed it then, you'll have another chance in 2061.

1988 - The movie *The Last Emperor* was nominated for nine Academy Awards and won all nine.

1990 – Customs officers in Middlesbrough, United Kingdom said they had seized what they believed was the barrel of a massive gun on a ship that was bound for Iraq.

1993 – Over 400 prisoners rioted at the Southern Ohio Correctional Facility in Lucasville, Ohio, and continued to do so for ten days, citing grievances related to prison conditions, as well as the forced vaccination of Nation of Islam prisoners (for tuberculosis) against their religious beliefs.

2000 – It was a day for commercialized ballparks in America. AT&T Park in San Francisco, Minute Maid Park in Houston, and Comerica Park in Detroit all held their opening ceremonies.

2006 – Iranian President Mahmoud Ahmadinejad announced that Iran had successfully enriched uranium.

2007 – Two bombings in the Algerian capital of Algiers, killed 33 people and wounded 222 others.

2008 – Babec, the first gorilla to have a pacemaker installed, was euthanized at the Birmingham Zoo in Birmingham, Alabama.

APRIL 12th

BIRTHDAYS FOR APRIL 12th

1777 Henry Clay; U.S. Secretary of State

1878 Lionel Barrymore; American actor

1916 Beverly Cleary; author

1916 Russ Garcia; musician, composer, orchestra leader

1919 Billy Vaughn; musician, orchestra leader

1923 Ann Miller; actress, dancer

1926 Jane Withers; actress

1932 Tiny Tim (Herbert Buckingham Khaury); entertainer

1936 Judy Lynn; singer

1940 Herbie Hancock; Oscar-winning jazz/fusion musician, composer

1940 John Hagee; American pastor and televangelist

1944 John Kay (Joachim Fritz Krauledat); guitarist, singer

1946 Ed O'Neill; actor

1947 Dan Lauria; actor

1947 Tom Clancy; author

1947 David Michael Letterman; TV host, comedian

1948 Sandra "Lois" Reeves; American singer

1949 Scott Turow; author

1950 David Cassidy; actor, singer

1952 Reuben Gant; football

1956 Alex Briley; singer

1956 Andy Garcia; actor

1957 Vince Gill; Grammy Award-winning singer

1958 Will Sergeant; musician, guitarist

1971 Shannen Doherty; actress

1979 Claire Danes; actress

EVENTS FOR APRIL 12th

1204 – The Crusaders of the Fourth Crusade breached the walls of Constantinople and entered the city, which they completely occupied the following day.

1606 - King James of England ordered a "Union Flag" combining the crosses of

As a result of the Broughton Suspension Bridge collapse, many bridges throughout England warn soldiers to break step before marching in formation. This sign appears at the entrance of the Albert Bridge in London. Public domain.

St. George of England and St. Andrew of Scotland.

1633 - Galileo was convicted of heresy for claiming the Earth orbited the sun and was not the center of the universe. He served three years under house arrest.

1831 – Soldiers marching on the Broughton Suspension Bridge in Manchester, England caused it to collapse. The collapse of the bridge is said to have been caused by a mechanical resonance induced by the troops marching over the bridge in step.

1861 - The United States Civil War began when Confederate troops attacked Fort Sumter in South Carolina.

1877 – James Alexander Tyng became the first baseball player to wear a catcher's mask.

1892 - Voters in Lockport, New York, became the first in the United States to use voting machines.

1905 - The Hippodrome in New York City opened with the gala musical, *A Yankee Circus on Mars*. Tickets were as low as 25 cents and as high as $2 for box seats. Believe it or not, the production cost a staggering $4 million.

Jim Tyng's baseball card, circa 1888. Note that this card was sponsored by a cigarette maker. Public domain.

1932 - *Joe Palooka* debuted on CBS radio and ran until August of that same year. The 15-minute series was heard on Tuesdays and Thursdays, and was sponsored by Heinz Rice Flakes.

1945 – U.S. President Franklin D. Roosevelt died from a stroke while in office; vice-president Harry Truman was sworn in as the 33rd President.

1954 – "Rock Around the Clock" was recorded by Bill Haley and the Comets.

Magazine cover photo of Jonas Salk taken by Yousuf Karsh specifically for *Wisdom Magazine*, 1956. Public domain.

1955 – Dr. Jonas Salk's polio vaccine was termed "safe, effective and potent" by the University of Michigan Polio Vaccine Evaluation Center.

1960 – Eric Peugeot, the youngest son of the founder of the Peugeot Corporation, was kidnapped in Paris. He was released on April 15th in exchange for $300,000 in ransom.

1961 - The Soviet Union launched the first man into space, cosmonaut Yuri Gargarin.

1963 – Martin Luther King, Jr., Ralph Abernathy, Fred Shuttlesworth and others were arrested in a Birmingham protest for "parading without a permit."

1964 - Arnold Palmer won his fourth Masters title and became the first golfer to earn career golf earnings of $506,496.84.

1967 – The Ahmanson Theatre opened in downtown Los Angeles.

1969 - Lucy and Snoopy, from the comic strip "Peanuts," were featured on the cover of *Saturday Review*.

1975 – Elton John's "Philadelphia Freedom" jumped into the #1 spot on *Billboard's* record charts, and stayed there for 2 weeks.

1980 - Liberian President William Tolbert was assassinated in a military coup. Samuel K. Doe was installed as the new head of state.

1981 - The world's first re-usable space shuttle *Columbia* was launched at Cape Canaveral.

1985 - Senator Joseph "Jake" Garn became the first politician in space when he lifted off aboard the Space Shuttle *Discovery* from the Kennedy Space Center in Florida.

1988 – Pop singer Sonny Bono was elected mayor of Palm Springs, California. He would later go on to serve in the U.S. House of Representatives.

1990 – Jim Gary's "Twentieth Century Dinosaurs" exhibition opened at the Smithsonian Institution National Museum of Natural History in Washington, D.C. The exhibit consisted

US Congressional portrait of Sonny Bono. Public domain.

entirely of colorful creations of dinosaurs made from discarded automobile parts.

1992 – The Euro Disney Resort officially opened with its theme park Euro Disneyland. The resort and its park's name were subsequently changed to "Disneyland Paris."

1994 – Laurence A. Canter and Martha S. Siegel posted the first commercial mass Usenet (an early version of the Internet) spam. The ads promoted a "Green card lottery," a government program designed to give "green cards" to certain non-citizens, allowing them to stay and work in the country.

1999 – US President Bill Clinton was cited for contempt of court for giving "intentionally false statements" in a sexual harassment civil lawsuit.

2002 – Pedro Carmona became interim President of Venezuela for one day during the military coup against Hugo Chávez.

2009 – U.S. Navy rescued Captain Richard Phillips, killing three pirates and capturing a fourth.

2010 – A train derailed near Merano, Italy, after running into a landslide, causing nine deaths and injuring 28 people.

APRIL 13th

BIRTHDAYS FOR APRIL 13th

1743 Thomas Jefferson; 3rd U.S. President, drafted the Declaration of Independence

1852 F.W. (Frank Winfield) Woolworth; merchant

1866 Butch Cassidy; old west outlaw

1919 Madalyn Murray O'Hair; American atheist activist

1923 Don Adams; American actor and comedian

1931 Dan Gurney; auto racer: Indianapolis Speedway Hall of Famer

1933 Ben Nighthorse Campbell; U.S. Senator

1935 Lyle Waggoner; actor

1937 Edward Fox; actor

1939 Paul Sorvino; actor

1942 Bill Conti; Academy Award-winning composer

1944 Jack Casady; musician, bassist

1944 Brian Pendleton; musician, guitarist

1945 Tony Dow; actor

1946 Al Green; singer, songwriter

1950 Ron Perlman; actor

1951 Max Weinberg; musician, drummer

1951 Peabo Bryson; singer

1954 Jimmy Destri; musician, organist

1957 Saundra Santiago; actress

1963 Garry Kasparov; World Chess Champion

1964 Caroline Rhea; Canadian actress

1964 David Love III; golfer

1970 Rick Schroder; actor

EVENTS FOR APRIL 13th

1059 - Pope Nicholas II issued a decree on the election of popes, declaring that only Cardinals would be allowed to elect them.

1598 – Henry IV of France issues the Edict of Nantes, allowing freedom of religion to the Huguenots (members of the Protestant Reformed Church of France). The Edict was repealed in 1685.

1742 - The first public performance of George Frideric Handel's *Messiah*

George Handel's actual signature. Public domain.

took place in Dublin, Ireland, in front of an audience of about 700.

1782 - Washington, North Carolina, was incorporated as the first town named for George Washington.

1796 - The first known elephant to come to the United States arrived from Bengal, India.

1829 - The English Parliament granted freedom of religion to Roman Catholics.

1849 - The Hungarian Republic was proclaimed.

1861 – After 34 hours of bombardment, Union forces at Ft. Sumter, off the coast of Charleston, South Carolina, surrendered to the Confederates.

1870 – The Metropolitan Museum of Art was founded in New York City.

1902 – James C. Penney opened his first store in Kemmerer, Wyoming.

1908 - A ban on dancing, card playing, and theater-attending was lifted by the New England Methodist Episcopal Conference.

The confederate flag flying over Fort Sumter. This image is a detail from a stereoscopic photograph taken by Alma A. Pelot on the morning of April 15, 1861.

1916 – The Funk Brothers Seed Company from Iowa sold Samuel Ramsay of Jacobsburg, Ohio the first hybrid seed corn for 15 cents a bushel.

1941 – The Soviet Union and Japan signed a neutrality pact.

1943 – On the 200th anniversary of Thomas Jefferson's birth, the Jefferson Memorial was dedicated in Washington, DC.

Construction of the Jefferson Memorial taken on May 15, 1941. Photo courtesy of the Faraday family.

1945 - Vienna, the first foreign capital to be occupied by Hitler, was liberated by the Russians under Fedor Tolbukhin.

1953 – CIA director Allen Dulles launched the program known as MKULTRA, the code name for a covert, illegal CIA human research program, run by the Office of Scientific Intelligence.

1953 - Ian Fleming published his first James Bond novel, *Casino Royale*.

1957 - Elvis Presley's "All Shook Up" rocketed to the #1 spot on *Billboard's* record charts and stayed there for two months.

1958 – At the age of 23, Van Cliburn from Kilgore, Texas was the first American to win 1st prize in the Soviet Union's Tchaikovsky International Piano Contest.

1963 – Sidney Poitier became the first African-American male to win the "Best Actor" award for *Lilies of the Field*.

Apollo 13's damaged Service Module, as photographed from the Command Module after being jettisoned.

1963 - Pete Rose got his first major-league hit for the Cincinnati Reds, a triple off Pittsburgh's Bob Friend.

1966 - Abdul Salam Arif, president of Iraq, was killed in a helicopter crash.

1970 – An oxygen tank aboard Apollo 13 exploded, putting the crew in great danger and causing major damage to the spacecraft while en route to the Moon.

1974 – Western Union (in cooperation with NASA and Hughes Aircraft) launched the United States' first commercial geosynchronous communications satellite, Westar 1.

1976 – The United States Treasury Department reintroduced the two-dollar bill as a Federal Reserve Note on Thomas Jefferson's 233rd birthday as part of the United States Bicentennial celebration.

Jefferson's portrait on the two-dollar bill. Public domain.

1980 - After 8 years, and 3,388 performances, Broadway's longest-running musical, *Grease*, closed, earning $8 million.

1981 - Janet Cook won a Pulitzer Prize for feature writing. Her piece, "Jimmy's World," was about an 8-year old heroin addict and it appeared in *The Washington Post*. Later the story was revealed to have been a completely fabricated.

1982 – "The Chicago Flood" occurred when the damaged wall of a utility tunnel beneath the Chicago River opened into a breach which flooded basements and underground facilities throughout the Chicago Loop with an estimated 250 million gallons of water.

1985 - After 60 years on radio, *The Grand Ole Opry* came to television.

1986 - Jack Nicklaus won his sixth Masters Tournament with a 9 under par 279.

1986 - Pope John Paul II officially visited the Synagogue of Rome; this was the first time a modern Pope has visited a synagogue.

1990 - The Soviet government officially accepted blame for the Katyn Massacre of World War II, when nearly 5,000 Polish military officers were murdered and buried in mass graves in the Katyn Forest.

1997 – At the age of 22 Tiger Woods became the youngest golfer to win golf's Masters Tournament.

2009 – Citi Field in Flushing, New York opened to almost 44,000 people in a game lost by the New York Mets 6-5 to the San Diego Padres.

APRIL 14th

BIRTHDAYS FOR APRIL 14th

1629 Christiaan Huygens; scientist, discovered the rings of Saturn

1866 Anne Sullivan; teacher for Helen Keller

1904 Sir John Gielgud; Emmy Award-winning actor

1925 Rod Steiger; Academy Award-winning actor

1926 Gloria Jean (Schoonover); actress

1932 Loretta Lynn; American country musician/singer

1934 Marty Keough; baseball

1935 Erich von Däniken; Swiss writer

1936 Bobby Nichols; golf

1936 Frank Serpico; American policeman

1941 Julie Christie; actress

1941 Pete (Peter Edward) Rose; baseball

1942 Dick Brooks; auto racer

1945 Ritchie Blackmore; musician, guitarist

1949 Dennis Bryon; musician, drummer

1949 John Shea; Emmy Award-winning actor

1950 Francis S. Collins; scientist, Nobel Peach Prize winner in 2000

1960 Brad Garrett; comedian, actor

1963 Cynthia Cooper; basketball

1964 Gina McKee; British actress

1966 David Justice; baseball

1966 Greg Maddux; baseball

1968 Anthony Michael Hall; actor

1977 Sarah Michelle Gellar; actress

1977 Chandra Levy; American intern

1996 Abigail Breslin; American actress

EVENTS FOR APRIL 14th

**The facade of the Cathedral of St. Peter and St. Paul.
Public domain.**

1434 – The foundation stone of Cathedral St. Peter and St. Paul in Nantes, France was laid.

1609 (or possibly 1610) - Count Gyorgy Thurzo made an investigative visit to Csejthe Castle in Hungary on orders from King Matthias and discovered Countess Elizabeth Bathory directing a torture session of young girls. Bathory was already infamous in the area for her torture and murder of servants and peasants, and her bloodthirsty activities have led many to cite her as one of the first vampires in history. Up until then her title and high-ranking relatives had made her untouchable.

1775 - The "Society for the Relief of Free Negroes Unlawfully Held in Bondage" was organized in Philadelphia by Benjamin Franklin and Benjamin Rush. This was the first known abolition society in North America.

1828 – Noah Webster placed a copyright on the first edition of his dictionary.

1865 – John Wilkes Booth, a well-known actor at the time, was allowed upstairs at Ford's Theatre; giving him access to United States President Abraham Lincoln's private box and the ability to kill the President.

The Presidential Box in Ford's Theatre, The Presidential Box in Ford's Theatre, where the 16th President of the United States, Abraham Lincoln, was shot by John Wilkes Booth. Today the theater functions as both a working theater and a museum. Photo taken by Matt H. Wade. Used by permission.

1894 - Thomas Edison demonstrated his kinetoscope. A viewer held 50 feet of film, about 13 seconds worth, that showed images of Annie Oakley and Buffalo Bill.

1912 - The British passenger liner RMS *Titanic* hit an iceberg in the North Atlantic, and sank the following morning with the loss of 1,517 lives.

1927 – The first Volvo automobile premiered in Gothenburg, Sweden.

1931 - Spain was declared a republic for the 2nd time after King Alfonso abdicated and fled the country.

1935 – "Black Sunday Storm," the worst dust storm of the U.S. Dust Bowl, rolled over Spearmen, Texas.

The ominous sight of a huge cloud of dust preparing to bury Spearman, Texas. Public domain.

1939 – *The Grapes of Wrath*, John Steinbeck's classic novel, was published by the Viking Press.

1954 – A Soviet spy ring in Australia was unveiled.

1955 – The Detroit Red Wings won the Stanley Cup for the 7th time in franchise history. Detroit wouldn't win the Cup again until 1997.

1956 - Videotape was first demonstrated at the 1956 NARTB (now NAB) convention in Chicago by Ampex. It was the demonstration of the first practical and commercially successful videotape format known as 2" Quadruplex. The machine cost $75,000, and was too large to fit in a small room.

1958 - Pianist Van Cliburn was presented on national television for the first time on NBC's *The Tonight Show* with Jack Parr.

1958 – The Soviet satellite Sputnik 2 fell from orbit after 162 days in orbit.

1960 - In New York City, the musical *Bye Bye Birdie* opened at the Martin Beck Theatre (now known as The Al Hirschfeld Theatre), starring Chita Rivera and Dick Van Dyke. It ran for 607 performances.

1962 – A Cuban military tribunal convicted 1,179 Bay of Pigs attackers and all were sentenced to 30 years in prison.

1969 – For the first time there was a tie for the Academy Award for "Best Actress" between Katharine Hepburn and Barbra Streisand.

1980 – The British heavy metal band Iron Maiden released their debut album, appropriately titled, *Iron Maiden*.

1981 - NASA's space shuttle *Columbia* made a perfect landing at Edwards Air Force Base after its maiden flight. The *Columbia* would make 27 more flights before its re-entry break-up in 2003.

1986 – Hailstones weighing more than two pounds fell on the Gopalganj district of Bangladesh, killing 92. To date, these were the heaviest hailstones ever recorded.

1988 – The USS *Samuel B. Roberts* ran into a mine in the Persian Gulf during Operation Earnest Will. The mine blew a 15-foot hole in the hull, flooded the engine room, and knocked the two gas turbines from their mounts. The blast also broke the keel of the ship; such structural damages are almost always fatal to most vessels. After 13 months of repairs, the *Roberts* was returned to service in a 1989 ceremony.

A port view of the guided missile frigate USS *SAMUEL B. ROBERTS* in dry dock in Dubai, UAE, for repairs. Public domain.

1989 - The U.S. government seized the Lincoln Savings and Loan Association in Irving, California. Charles Keating (for whom the Keating Five were named – John McCain among them) eventually went to jail as part of the massive 1980s Savings and Loan Crisis which costs U.S. taxpayers nearly $200 billion in bailouts, and many people their life savings.

1991 – Thieves stole 20 paintings worth $500 million from the Van Gogh Museum in Amsterdam. The missing artwork was found less than an hour later in an abandoned car near the museum.

1994 - Two United States F-15 fighter planes shot down two American helicopters over northern Iraq killing 26, in what the Pentagon called "a tragic accident."

1997 – Erich Priebke, former SS Captain was finally retried; on July 22nd he was sentenced to five years in prison for his war crimes.

1999 – NATO mistakenly bombed a convoy of ethnic Albanian refugees – Yugoslav officials said 75 people were killed.

1999 – A severe hailstorm struck Sydney, Australia causing $2.3 billion in insured damages, the most costly natural disaster in Australian history.

2000 – Metallica drummer Lars Ulrich filed a lawsuit against P2P sharing phenomenon Napster. This law-suit eventually led the movement against file-sharing programs.

2002 – Venezuelan President Hugo Chavez returned to office two days after being ousted and arrested by the country's military.

2003 – "The Human Genome Project," a project to understand the genetic makeup of the human species, was completed with 99% of the human genome sequenced to an accuracy of 99.99%.

2003 – U.S. troops in Baghdad captured Abu Abbas, leader of the Palestinian group that killed an American, on the hijacked cruise liner the MS *Achille Lauro* in 1985.

2005 – The Oregon Supreme Court nullified marriage licenses issued to gay couples a year earlier by Multnomah County.

2007 – At least 200,000 demonstrators in Ankara, Turkey protest against the possible candidacy of incumbent Prime Minister Recep Tayyip Erdoğan.

2010 – Volcanic ash from one of several eruptions beneath Eyjafjallajökull, an ice cap in Iceland, began disrupting air traffic across northern and western Europe.

APRIL 15th

BIRTHDAYS FOR APRIL 15th

1452 Leonardo da Vinci; Painter, sculptor, architect, and engineer

1684 Catherine I of Russia

1741 Charles Wilson Peale; artist

1841 Joseph E. Seagram; Canadian distillery founder

1843 Henry James; author

1892 Corrie ten Boom; Dutch author and Holocaust survivor

1894 Nikita Khrushchev; Premier of the Soviet Union

1922 Harold Washington; Chicago Mayor

1930 Herb Pomeroy; musician, trumpeter, teacher, bandleader

1933 David Hamilton; British photographer, film director and producer

1933 Elizabeth Montgomery; actress

1933 Roy Clark; musician, guitarist, banjo player, entertainer, singer

1933 Mel Kenyon; auto racer

1937 Bob Luman; singer

1940 Willie (William Henry) Davis; baseball

1940 Woody (Woodrow Thompson) Fryman; baseball

1942 Walt Hazzard; basketball

1942 Julie Sommars; actress

1942 Kenneth Lay; American businessman

1944 Dave Edmunds; Welsh musician

1945 Ted Sizemore; baseball

1947 Linda Bloodworth-Thomason; producer, writer

1948 Victor Regalado; golf

1950 Dick (Richard Louis) Sharon; baseball

1950 Amy Wright; actress

1951 Heloise (Poncé Kiah Marchelle Heloise Cruse Evans); newspaper columnist, writer

1954 Seka (Dorothea Patton); American pornographic actress

1955 Dodi Al-Fayed; Egyptian businessman

1956 Michael Cooper; basketball

1957 Evelyn Ashford; Olympic gold medalist, track

1962 Tom Kane; American voice actor

1966 Graeme Clark; musician, bassist

1966 Samantha Fox; singer

1971 Jason Sehorn; football

1972 Lou Romano; American voice actor

1976 Susan Ward; American actress

1982 Seth Rogen; Canadian actor and writer

1990 Emma Watson; English actress

EVENTS FOR APRIL 15th

1450 - The French defeated the English at the "Battle of Formigny" in the last phase of the 100 Years' War.

1755 - Dr. Samuel Johnson, English poet, journalist and lexicographer, published *A Dictionary of the English Language*.

1834 - President Andrew Jackson signed the first presidential protest. He protested against a Senate resolution drawn up against him.

1965 – President Abraham Lincoln succumbed to a gunshot wound inflicted by an assassin the night before; he was pronounced dead at 7:22 am.

1865 - Andrew Johnson became the 17th president of the United States following the death of Abraham Lincoln.

1892 - The General Electric Company was formed.

1912 – The British passenger liner, the RMS *Titanic*, sank in the North Atlantic at 2:20 a.m., two and a half hours after hitting an iceberg. More than a thousand people died.

News of the *Titanic* as it appeared in The New York Herald. Public domain.

1923 - Insulin, discovered the previous year, became generally available for people with diabetes.

1924 - Rand McNally published its first road atlas.

1923 - Dr. Lee DeForest's "Phonofilm," the first sound-on-sound motion picture film, was demonstrated at New York City's Rivoli Theatre.

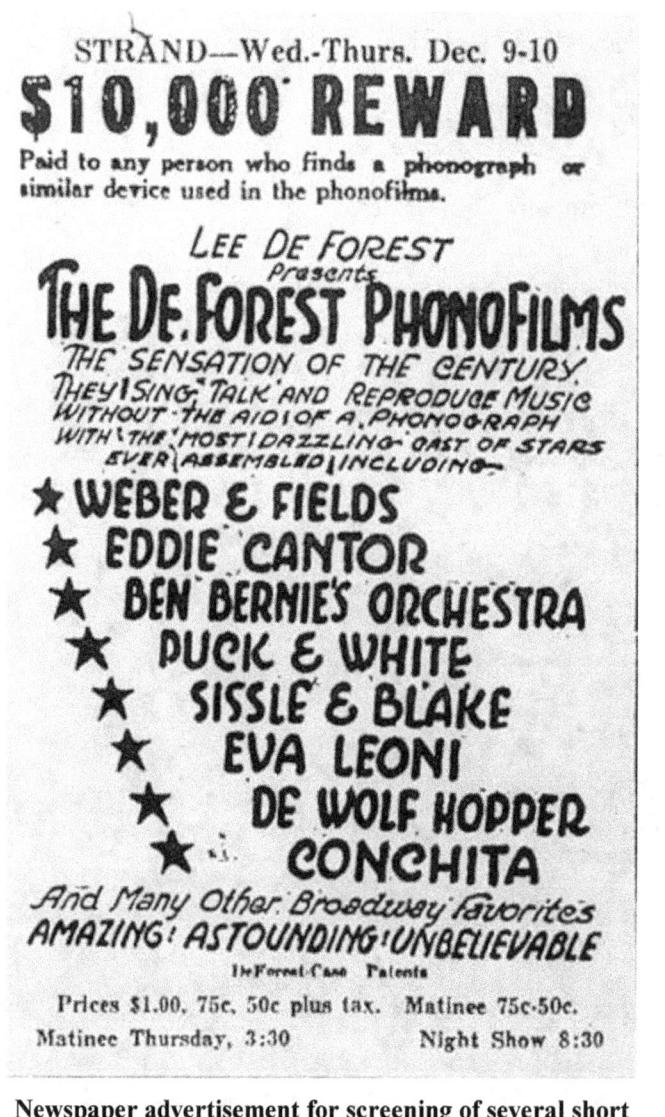

Newspaper advertisement for screening of several short films produced by DeForest Phonofilms at the Strand Theater of Biloxi, Mississippi. The reward mentioned was offered as "proof" that no phonograph was used for the sound. Photo courtesy of the Library of Congress.

1934 - Comic strip characters, Dagwood and Blondie Bumstead welcomed a baby boy named "Baby Dumpling." The baby would later be renamed as "Alexander."

1947 – Jackie Robinson debuted for the Brooklyn Dodgers.

1952 – The United States B-52 Stratofortress flew for the first time.

1955 – Ray Kroc opened the first franchised McDonald's restaurant in Des Plaines, Illinois.

1958 - The San Francisco Giants beat the Los Angeles Dodgers 8–0 at San Francisco's Seals Stadium, in the first Major League Baseball regular season game ever played in California.

1967 - Massive parades to protest Vietnam policy were held in New York City and San Francisco. In New York, police estimated that 100,000 to 125,000 people listened to speeches by Martin Luther King, Jr., Floyd McKissick, Stokely Carmichael, and Dr. Benjamin Spock. Prior to the march, nearly 200 draft cards were burned by youths in Central Park. In San Francisco, black nationalists led a march, but most of the 20,000 marchers were white.

1968 - Two unmanned Soviet satellites, Cosmos 212 and 213, found each other and docked automatically while in Earth's orbit.

1983 – The first Disney theme park to be built outside of the United States opened in Tokyo.

A floral arrangement depicting Disney Character Stitch greeting the visitors to Tokyo Disneyland. Public Domain.

1985 – South Africa ended its ban on interracial marriages.

1986 – The United States launched "Operation El Dorado Canyon," its bombing raids against Libyan targets in response to a bombing in West Germany that killed two U.S. servicemen.

1989 – A human crush occurs at Hillsborough Stadium, home of Sheffield Wednesday, in the FA Cup Semi Final, resulting in the deaths of 96 Liverpool F.C. fans.

1990 - Retired screen beauty Greta Garbo died from kidney disease at age 84.

1996 - South Africa's "Truth and Reconciliation Commission," looking into abuses during the apartheid era, began its public hearings.

1999 - It was announced in Boston that a lost song from Gilbert and Sullivan's classic operetta *H.M.S. Pinafore* was discovered by a Holy Cross professor.

2002 – An Air China Boeing 767-200, flight CA129 crashed into a hillside during heavy rain and fog near Busan, South Korea, killing 128.

2010 – Volcanic ash from the eruption of Eyjafjallajökull in Iceland continued to lead to the closure of airspace over most of Europe.

BIRTHDAYS FOR APRIL 16*th*

1867 Wilbur Wright; aviator

1889 Sir Charlie Chaplin; Actor

1917 Barry Nelson (Nielsen); actor

1921 Peter Ustinov; Academy Award-winning actor

1924 Henry Mancini; Academy Award-winning composer

1928 "Night Train" Lane; American football player

1929 Roy Hamilton; singer

1930 Herbie Mann (Soloman); jazz musician, flautist

1931 Edie Adams (Elizabeth Edith Enke); singer, actress

1933 Ike Pappas; newsman

1935 Bobby Vinton (Stanley Robert Vinton, Jr.); singer

1939 Dusty Springfield (Mary Isobel Catherine Bernadette O'Brien); singer

1942 Jim Lonborg; baseball

1947 Kareem Abdul-Jabbar (Lew Alcindor); basketball

1947 Gerry Rafferty; singer, songwriter

1953 Jay O. Sanders; actor

1954 Ellen Barkin; actress

1963 Jimmy Osmond; singer

1965 Jon Cryer; actor

1965 Martin Lawrence; actor

1968 Vickie Guerrero; American professional wrestling personality

1976 Lukas Haas; actor

EVENTS FOR APRIL 16th

73 - Masada, a Jewish fortress, fell to the Romans after several months of siege, ending the Jewish Revolt.

1071 - Bari fell to Robert Guiscard, ending Byzantine rule in Italy.

1346 - The Serbian Empire was proclaimed in Skopje by Dusan Silni, occupying much of the Balkans.

1582 - Spanish conquistador Hernando de Lerma founded the settlement of Salta, Argentina.

1746 - The Battle of Culloden was fought between the French-supported Jacobites and the British Hanoverian forces commanded by William Augustus, Duke of Cumberland.

1780 – The University of Münster in Münster, North Rhine-Westphalia, Germany was founded.

1799 - Napoleon drove Ottoman Turks across the River Jordan near Acre during the Battle of Mount Tabor.

1853 - The first passenger rail opened in India, from Bori Bunder, Bombay, to Thane.

1862 - The Battle at Lee's Mills in Virginia became a pivotal point of The Battle of Yorktown.

1862 - A bill ending slavery in the District of Columbia became law.

1863 - Ships led by Union Admiral David Dixon Porter move through heavy Confederate artillery fire on approach to Vicksburg, Mississippi.

1881 – The legendary Bat Masterson fought his final gunfight. It happened in Dodge City, Kansas and, believe it or not, he survived. He just didn't fight anymore. He lived until 1921 when he died of a heart attack while sitting at his desk.

1912 - Harriet Quimby became the first woman to fly an airplane across the English Channel.

1917 - Vladimir Lenin returned to Petrograd from exile in Finland.

Deputies Bat Masterson (standing) and Wyatt Earp in Dodge City, 1876. The scroll on Earp's chest is a cloth pin-on badge. Public domain.

1919 - Mahatma Gandhi organized a day of "prayer and fasting" in response to the British slaughter of Indian protesters in the Amritsar Massacre.

1922 - The Treaty of Rapallo, in which Germany and the Soviet Union re-established diplomatic relations between Berlin and Moscow, was signed.

1925 - During the Communist St. Nedelya Church assault in Sofia, 150 were killed and another 500 were wounded.

1941 - The Italian convoy *Duisburg*, directed to Tunisia, was attacked and destroyed by British ships.

1941 - Bob Feller of the Cleveland Indians threw the first (and to date, the only) opening day no-hitter in the history of Major League Baseball, beating the Chicago White Sox 1-0.

1943 - Dr. Albert Hofmann discovered the psychedelic effects of LSD.

1945 - The Red Army began the final assault on German forces around Berlin.

1945 - The United States Army liberated the Nazi Sonderlager (high security) Prisoner of War camp Oflag IV-C (better known as Colditz Castle).

1945 - More than 7,000 people died when the German refugee ship *Goya* was sunk by a Soviet submarine torpedo.

Parking lot 1/4 of a mile away from the explosion. Courtesy of Special Collections, University of Houston Libraries.

1946 - Syria gained independence.

1947 – The Texas City Disaster was the deadliest industrial accident in U.S. history. The incident began with a mid-morning fire on board the French-registered vessel SS *Grandcamp* in the Port of Texas City. The fire detonated approximately 2,300 tons of ammonium nitrate and the resulting chain reaction of fires and explosions killed at least 581 people.

1947 - Bernard Baruch coined the term "Cold War" (in reference to post–World War II geopolitical tensions) to describe the relationship between the United States and the Soviet Union.

1953 - Queen Elizabeth II launched the Royal Yacht *Britannia*.

1953 – President Eisenhower delivered his "Chance for Peace" speech to the National Association of Newspaper Editors.

1955 - The Burma-Japanese peace treaty signed in Rangoon on November 5, 1954 went into force, and formally ended their state of war.

1963 - Dr. Martin Luther King, Jr. wrote his famous *Letter from Birmingham Jail* while incarcerated in Birmingham, Alabama for protesting against segregation.

1964 – The Rolling Stones released their debut album titled, appropriately, *The Rolling Stones*.

1972 – The 5th trip to send man to the moon was underway as Apollo 16 launched from Cape Canaveral, Florida. While they were on the moon they set a land speed record by driving the lunar rover at the break-neck speed of 11 miles per hour.

1976 – As a measure to curb population growth, the minimum age for marriage in India was raised to 21 years for men and 18 years for women.

1977 - Better known as Detective Kenneth "Hutch" Hutchison from the TV series *Starsky & Hutch*, David Soul enjoyed fame as a pop music star. His release, "Don't Give Up On Us, Baby," reached the #1 position on *Billboard's* Hot 100 Chart.

1987 - British Conservative MP Harvey Proctor appeared at the Bow Street Magistrates' Court in London charged with gross indecency.

1988 - In Forlì, Italy, Red Brigades killed Italian Senator Roberto Ruffilli, an advisor to Prime Minister Ciriaco de Mita.

1990 - The "Doctor of Death," Jack Kevorkian, performed his first assisted suicide.

1992 - The *Katina P.* ran aground off of Maputo, Mozambique. Sixty-thousand tons of crude oil spilled into the ocean.

2003 - The Treaty of Accession was signed in Athens admitting 10 new member states to the European Union.

Queen Mary 2, leaving Southampton on her maiden voyage. Photo by George Hutchinson. Used by permission.

2004 – The super liner *Queen Mary 2* embarked on her first Trans-Atlantic crossing, linking the golden age of ocean travel to the modern age of ocean travel.

2007 - Seung-Hui Cho, shot 32 people to death and injured 23 others before committing suicide during the Virginia Tech massacre.

APRIL 17th

BIRTHDAYS FOR APRIL 17th

1741 Samuel Chase; Signer of the Declaration of Independence, Justice of the U.S. Supreme Court

1837 J.P. Morgan; financier

1896 Señor Wences; Spanish ventriloquist

1897 Thornton Wilder; Pulitzer Prize-winning novelist

1903 Gregor Piatigorsky; cellist, teacher

1918 William Holden (Beedle, Jr.); Academy Award-winning actor

1923 Harry Reasoner; newsman

1929 James Last; German band leader

1934 Don Kirshner; music publisher

1948 Jan Hammer; Czech composer

1950 Pedro Garcia; baseball

1951 Olivia Hussey; actress

1954 Rowdy Roddy Piper (Roderick George Toombs); professional wrestler

1954 Michael Sembello; American musician

1955 Pete Shelley (McNeish); musician, singer

1959 Sean Bean; actor

1961 Boomer Esiason; football

1964 Lela Rochon; actress

1967 Liz Phair; singer, songwriter

1974 Victoria Beckham; English singer (Spice Girls)

EVENTS FOR APRIL 17th

69 – After the First Battle of Bedriacum, Vitellius became Roman Emperor.

1397 – Geoffrey Chaucer told the *Canterbury Tales* for the first time at the court of Richard II. Chaucer scholars have also identified this date (in 1387) as when the book's pilgrimage to Canterbury began.

1492 – Spain and Christopher Columbus signed a contract for him to sail to Asia to get spices.

1521 – Martin Luther spoke to the assembly at the Diet of Worms, and refused to recant his teachings.

1524 – Giovanni da Verrazzano (Italian explorer of North America, in the service of the French crown) reached New York harbor.

1555 – After 18 months of siege, Siena surrendered to the Florentine-Imperial army; the Republic of Siena was incorporated into the Grand Duchy of Tuscany.

1797 – Sir Ralph Abercromby attacked San Juan, Puerto Rico, in what became one of the largest invasions to Spanish territories in America.

1861 – Virginia seceded from the United States.

1864 – The Battle of Plymouth began when Confederate forces attacked Plymouth, North Carolina.

1865 – Mary Surratt was arrested as a conspirator in the assassination of Abraham Lincoln. Sentenced to death by hanging, she was the first woman executed by the United States federal government.

1895 – The Treaty of Shimonoseki between China and Japan was signed. This marked the end of the First Sino-Japanese War, and the defeated Qing Empire was forced to renounce its claims on Korea and to concede the southern portion of the Fengtien province, Taiwan, and the Pescadores Islands to Japan.

1905 – The Supreme Court of the United States decided Lochner v. New York, which held that the "right to free contract" was implicit in the due process clause of the 14th Amendment of the United States Constitution. The result of this finding was the freedom of individuals and corporations to form contracts without government restrictions.

1907 – The Ellis Island immigration center processed 11,747 people, a record number for one day.

1924 – Metro-Goldwyn-Mayer studios was formed from a merger of Metro Pictures, Goldwyn Pictures, and the Louis B. Mayer Company.

Ellis Island's Immigrant Landing Station as it stood in 1905. Public domain.

1941 – During World War II, the Kingdom of Yugoslasvia surrendered to Germany.

1942 – POW French General Henri Giraud escaped from his castle prison in Festung Königstein.

1949 – At midnight 26 Irish counties officially left the British Commonwealth. A 21-gun salute on the O'Connell Bridge, Dublin, ushered in the Republic of Ireland.

1955 - Imre Nagy, the communist Premier of Hungary, was ousted for being too moderate.

1958 – King Baudouin of Belgium officially opened the World Fair in Brussels, also known as Expo '58.

1960 – Russwood Park, a baseball stadium in Memphis, Tennessee, burned to the ground from a fire shortly after a pre-season exhibition game between the Chicago White Sox and the Cleveland Indians. The cause of the fire remains officially unknown.

1961 – A group of CIA financed and trained Cuban refugees landed at the Bay of Pigs in Cuba with the aim of ousting Fidel Castro. The invasion, launched less than three months after John F. Kennedy assumed the United States' Presidency, failed to meat its objective.

This is Mustang Serial #1, produced in 1964, titled as a 1964 ½ Mustang due to the fact that the first Mustangs did not come out until the middle of the year. Public domain.

1964 – The Ford Motor Company unveiled the Ford Mustang at the New York World's Fair.

1964 – Jerrie Mock becomes the first woman to fly solo around the world.   The trip took 29 days, 21 stopovers and almost 22,860 miles, and was done entirely in a Cessna 180.

1964 – Shea Stadium opened and would be the home for the New York Mets for more than 40 years.

1969 – Sirhan Sirhan was convicted of assassinating Robert F. Kennedy and was sentenced to life in prison.

1969 – Czechoslovakian Communist Party chairman Alexander Dubček was deposed.

1970 – After an in-flight explosion, the crew of Apollo 13 safely returned to earth.

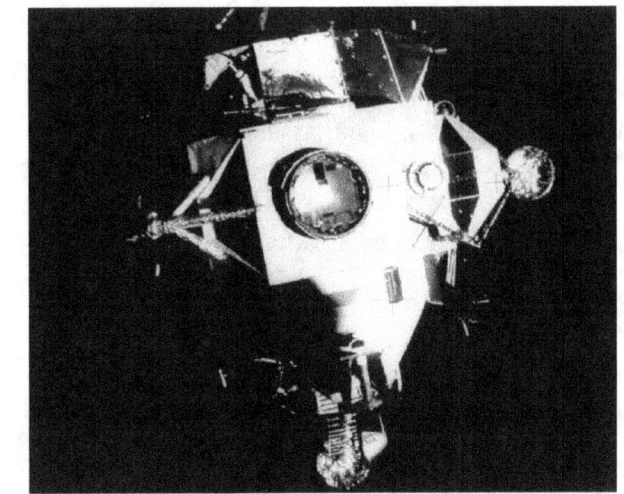

1971 – The People's Republic of Bangladesh formed under Sheikh Mujibur Rahman at Mujibnagor.

The Apollo 13 Lunar Module *Aquarius* was jettisoned above the Earth after serving as a lifeboat for four days. It eventually reentered Earth's atmosphere over Fiji and burned up. This photo was taken by one of the astronauts on board the Command Module Odyssey. Public domain.

1971 – Sierra Leone became a republic.

1972 - The Boston Marathon allowed women to officially compete for the first time. The first woman to run the marathon's entire length was Roberta "Bobbi" Gibb who accomplished her feat six years earlier. Since she was not officially allowed to run, Roberta had to complete the course without wearing a number.

1973 – German counter-terrorist unit GSG 9 was founded.

1973 - Federal Express officially began operations with the launch of 14 small aircraft from Memphis International Airport. On that night, Federal Express delivered 186 packages to 25 U.S. cities from Rochester, New York, to Miami, Florida.

1975 – The Cambodian Civil War ended. The Khmer Rouge captured the capital Phnom Penh and the Cambodian government forced surrender.

1979 - Schoolchildren in the Central African Republic were arrested (and around 100 killed) for protesting against compulsory school uniforms. An African judicial commission later determined that Emperor Jean-Bédel Bokassa "almost certainly" took part in the massacre.

1982 – Patriation of the Canadian constitution in Ottawa became law by Proclamation of Queen Elizabeth II, Queen of Canada.

1984 – Police Constable Yvonne Fletcher was killed by gunfire from the Libyan People's Bureau in London during a small demonstration outside the embassy and ten others were wounded. The events led to an 11-day siege of the building.

1986 - The "Hindawi Affair" began when an Irishwoman was found unknowingly carrying explosives onto an El Al flight from London to Tel Aviv. She had been given the bag by her fiancé, Nezar Hindawi, a Jordanian, believing he had sent her on the flight for the purpose of meeting his parents before marriage. She claimed no knowledge of the contents.

1986 – "The Three Hundred and Thirty Five Years' War" between the Netherlands and the Isles of Scilly came to an end.

1991 - The Dow Jones Industrial Average closed above 3,000 for the first time ever, at 3,004.46.

1993 - Laurence Powell and Stacey Koon were found guilty of violating Rodney King's civil rights and sentenced to 30 months in prison. The officers had been acquitted of charges of assault with a deadly weapon the year previous.

APRIL 18th

BIRTHDAYS FOR APRIL 18th

1857 Clarence Darrow; attorney

1882 Leopold Stokowski; conductor

1922 Barbara Hale; actress

1924 Clarence "Gatemouth" Brown; American musician

1941 Walt Sweeney; football

1941 Mike Vickers; musician, guitarist, reed instrumentalist

1942 Steve Blass; baseball

1942 Pete Gogolak; football

1942 Jochen Rindt; auto racer

1946 Hayley Mills; actress

1946 Alexander "Skip" Spence; musician, guitarist, singer

1947 Dorothy Lyman; actress

1947 James Woods; actor

1953 Rick Moranis; actor

1956 John James; actor

1956 Eric Roberts; actor

1961 Jane Leeves; actress

1962 Wilber Buddyhia Marshall; football

1963 Conan O'Brien; TV talk show host, Emmy Award-winning writer

1963 Eric McCormack; actor

1967 Maria Bello; actress

1976 Melissa Joan Hart; actress

EVENTS FOR APRIL 18th

1506 – The cornerstone of the current St. Peter's Basilica was placed into position.

St. Peter's Basilica, believed to be the burial site of St. Peter, seen from the River Tiber. Public domain.

1775 - Paul Revere and other riders rode from Charlestown to Lexington to warn of the arrival of British troops at the start of the American Revolution.

1783 – The fighting ceased in the American Revolution, eight years to the day after it began.

1846 - R.E. House of New York City patented the telegraph ticker (at the time referred to as a "Magnetic Letter Printing Telegraph").

1881 – Billy the Kid escaped from the Lincoln County jail in Mesilla, New Mexico.

San Francisco Earthquake of 1906: Stockton Street from Union Square, looking toward Market Street. Public domain.

LA Times **article criticizing the behavior of the revivalists at Azusa Street. Public domain.**

1906 – The city of San Francisco, California, was struck by an enormous earthquake shortly after five in the morning. It is said to have been a 7.9 quake.

1906 – The *Los Angeles Times* story on the Azusa Street Revival launched Pentecostalism as a worldwide movement.

1909 - Fifteenth century French heroine Joan of Arc was beatified in a ceremony at the Vatican.

1912 – The Cunard liner RMS *Carpathia* brought 705 survivors from the RMS *Titanic* to New York City.

1923 – Yankee Stadium, dubbed by the press as "The House that Ruth Built," opened its gates to the general public. In its opening day game, the Yankees defeated the Red Sox 4-1.

1924 - The first *Crossword Puzzle Book* was published by Simon and Schuster, Inc.

1934 - J.F. Cantrell opened the first "washateria" in Fort Worth, Texas, the first Laundromat. He offered four washing machines that he rented by the hour, but he had no dryers.

1942 - In World War II, U.S. aircraft commanded by James Doolittle bombed Tokyo for the first time as well as Yokohama and Nagoya.

1949 - An Act of the Irish Parliament declared Ireland to be a republic

1955 – The man who discovered the theory of general relativity, Albert Einstein, died in New Jersey.

1956 - Prince Rainier III of Monaco married Hollywood screen actress, Grace Kelly, in a civil ceremony (a religious ceremony was held the following day). She retired from films after becoming princess of the small country.

1966 - *The Academy Awards* ceremony was telecast in color for the first time. The award for Best Picture that year went to *The Sound of Music*.

1968 – The London Bridge was sold to American Robert McCullough for 2.4 million dollars. This bridge was actually the second bridge to bear the name, and when it fell into disrepair the

Photo of the reconstructed London Bridge in Lake Havasu, Arizona. Photo taken by Aran Johnson, used by permission.

Common Council of the City of London put it up for sale. It was later re-erected in Arizona.

1978 - The U.S. Senate voted 68–32 to turn the Panama Canal over to Panamanian control by December 31, 1999.

1980 - Rhodesia gained legal independence as Zimbabwe under President Canaan Banana.

1981 - The Pawtucket Red Sox and Rochester Red Wings, two teams from the Triple-A International League, played the longest game to date in professional baseball. The 33 innings of play lasted for eight hours and 25 minutes from April 18th and 19th and then resumed on June 23rd at McCoy Stadium in Pawtucket, Rhode Island. Pawtucket won 3-2.

1983 - A suicide bomb shattered the United States embassy in Beirut and killed at least 63 people.

1984 - Michael Jackson went under the knife in Los Angeles, California, as doctors performed scalp surgery to repair damage caused by a fire in a Pepsi commercial.

1988 - An Israeli court convicted John Demjanjuk of Nazi war crimes, saying he was the gas chamber operator known as "Ivan The Terrible" in World War II.

1996 - More than 100 Lebanese refugees were killed when Israeli artillery shells ripped into a crowded United Nations peacekeepers base where they were sheltering.

1997 – The Red River of the North broke through dikes and flooded Grand Forks, North Dakota and East Grand Forks, Minnesota, causing more than $2 billion in damage.

1999 – After more than 20 years, Wayne Gretzky retired from professional hockey.

2007 – The Supreme Court of the United States upheld the Partial-Birth Abortion Ban Act in a 5-4 decision.

APRIL 19th

BIRTHDAYS FOR APRIL 19th

1721 Roger Sherman; statesman, Signer of the Declaration of Independence

1832 Lucretia Garfield; wife of James Garfield, 20th US President

1903 Eliot Ness; American lawman

1905 Tommy Benford; musician, drummer

1920 Frank Fontaine; comedian, actor, singer

1925 Hugh O'Brian; actor

1930 Dick Sargent (Richard Cox); actor

1931 Alex Webster; football

1933 Jayne Mansfield; actress

1934 Dickie Goodman; entertainer

1935 Dudley Moore; actor

1936 Wilfried Martens; Belgium Prime Minister

1937 Elinor Donahue; actress

1941 Alan Price; musician, keyboardist, singer

1941 Bobby Russell; American songwriter

1942 Larry Ramos; musician, guitarist, singer

1943 Eve Graham; singer

1946 Tim Curry; actor

1947 Mark Volman; musician, saxophonist, singer

1949 Paloma Picasso; fashion designer, daughter of artist Pablo Picasso

1956 Sue Barker; tennis

1960 Frank John Viola, Jr.; baseball

1962 Al Unser, Jr.; Indy Car national champion

1968 Ashley Judd; actress

1979 Kate Hudson; actress

1981 Hayden Christensen; Canadian actor

EVENTS FOR APRIL 19th

1587 - English Admiral Sir Francis Drake entered Cadiz harbor and sank the Spanish fleet, an action he referred to "as singeing the King of Spain's beard."

1713 - With no living male heirs, Charles VI, Holy Roman Emperor, issued the Pragmatic Sanction of 1713 to ensure that Habsburg and the Austrian throne would be inherited by his daughter, Maria Theresa of Austria (not actually born until 1717).

1775 - The first battle of the American Revolutionary War started when British and American soldiers exchanged fire in Lexington and Concord.

1824 – Poet George Gordon, a.k.a. "Lord Byron", died at age 36.

1839 - The Treaty of London was signed, establishing recognition of the Kingdom of Belgium by all the states of Europe.

1850 - The Clayton-Bulwer agreement was signed under which Britain and the United States agreed not to obtain exclusive control of a proposed Panama Canal.

1897 - The first Boston Marathon was held in Boston, Massachusetts. John J. McDermott of New York ran the 24.5-mile course of the all-male event in a winning time of 2:55:10.

1919 – Leslie Leroy Irvin of the United States made the first successful voluntary free-fall parachute jump using a new kind of self-contained parachute.

1927 – Mae West was sentenced to 10 days in jail for obscenity for her play *Sex*. The sentence was imposed despite the fact that 325,000 people had watched it, including members of the police department and their wives, judges of the criminal courts, and seven members of the district attorney's staff.

1933 - President Franklin D. Roosevelt issued a proclamation removing the United States from the gold standard.

1943 – Polish Jews rose up in the Warsaw ghetto in a failed rebellion against the Nazis.

Photo from Jürgen Stroop's report to Heinrich Himmler from May 1943. The original German caption: "Forcibly pulled out of dug-outs." Public domain.

1943 – Swiss chemist Dr. Albert Hofmann deliberately took LSD for the first time.

1945 - Rodgers and Hammerstein's musical *Carousel* opened on Broadway. It was an immediate hit with both critics and audiences.

1951 - General Douglas MacArthur gave his famous speech in which he said, "Old soldiers never die, they just fade away."

1955 – The German automaker Volkswagen, after six years of selling cars in the United States, founded Volkswagen of America in Englewood Cliffs, New Jersey, to standardize its dealer and service network.

1956 - British diver Lionel Crabb dived into Portsmouth harbor (on the south coast of England) to investigate a visiting Soviet cruiser, vanished and was presumed dead.

1960 – A student uprising toppled the authoritarian government of South Korean President Syngman Rhee.

1961 – The Bay of Pigs invasion of Cuba ended in success for the Cuban government.

Syngman Rhee in 1956. Public domain.

1971 – Russia launched its space station *Salyut* into earth's orbit.

1971 – Charles Manson was sentenced to death for the Sharon Tate murders.

USSR stamp, Memories of cosmonauts aboard Salyut 1. Public domain.

1975 – India launched Aryabhata, their first satellite.

1984 – "Advance Australia Fair" was proclaimed as Australia's national anthem, and green and gold as the national colors.

1985 – The FBI began their siege on the compound of "The Covenant, The Sword, and the Arm of the Lord" (CSAL), a radical Christian group in Arkansas. Although no proof was ever offered, suspicions still persist that they were somehow tied to the Oklahoma City bombing which occurred ten years to the date later.

1987 – *The Simpsons* premiered as a short cartoon on *The Tracey Ullman Show.*

1989 – Forty-seven crewmen died in an explosion on the United States battleship USS *Iowa* during Atlantic maneuvers.

**Heavy smoke pouring from USS *Iowa's* #2 Turret following an internal explosion.
Pubic domain.**

1989 - Trisha Meili was attacked while jogging in New York City's Central Park; as her identity remained secret for years, she became known as the "Central Park Jogger."

1990 – The television show *Wings* premiered on NBC.

1993 - The Branch-Davidian's compound in Waco, Texas, burned to the ground after a 51-day standoff.

1993 - South Dakota governor George Mickelson and seven others were killed when a state-owned aircraft crashed in Iowa.

1995 – The Alfred P. Murrah Federal Building in Oklahoma City, Oklahoma, USA, was bombed, killing 168. That same day convicted murderer Richard Wayne Snell, who had ties to one of the bombers, Timothy McVeigh, was executed in Arkansas.

1999 – The German Bundestag, the lower house of the bicameral parliament of Germany, returned to Berlin.

President William J. Clinton
Eulogy for Bombing Victims
Oklahoma City, Oklahoma
April 23, 1995

My fellow Americans:

Today our nation is joined with you in grief. We mourn with you. We share your hope against hope that others have survived. We thank all who have worked so heroically to save lives and solve this crime. We pledge to do all we can to help you heal the injured, to rebuild this city, and to bring to justice those who did this evil deed.

A part of President Bill Clinton's address to the victims of the Oklahoma City Bombing terrorist attack made four days after the bombing. Image provided by the National Archives and Records Administration.

2005 – Cardinal Joseph Ratzinger was elected Pope Benedict XVI on the second day of the Papal conclave.

2008 – Bowie Seamount, an underwater volcano off the coast of British Columbia, Canada became a Marine Protected Area because of the rich ecosystem it supports.

BIRTHDAYS FOR APRIL 20th

1889 Adolf Hitler; Nazi dictator

1893 Harold Lloyd; comedian, actor

1908 Lionel Hampton; American musician

1920 John Paul Stevens; U.S. Supreme Court Associate Justice

1923 Mother Angelica; American nun and broadcaster

1923 Tito Puente; jazz musician, bandleader

1929 Bob Braun; television personality

1936 Pat Roberts; U.S. Senator

1937 George Takei; actor

1939 Johnny Tillotson; singer

1941 Ryan O'Neal; actor

1945 Michael Brandon; actor

1945 Steve Spurrier; football

1945 Jimmy Winston; musician, organist

1946 Tommy Hutton; baseball

1947 Brian Lavender; hockey

1947 David Leland; actor, director, writer

1948 Craig Frost; musician, keyboardist

1948 Joe Bonner; pianist, composer

1949 Jessica Lange; Academy Award-winning actress

1951 Luther Vandross; singer, songwriter

1955 Don Pettit; American astronaut and inventor

1959 Clint Howard; actor

1961 Don Mattingly; baseball

1964 Crispin Glover; actor

1972 Carmen Electra; actress

1976 Joey Lawrence; actor

1980 Chris Duffy; baseball

EVENTS FOR APRIL 20th

1657 – Freedom of religion was granted to the Jews of New Amsterdam (later called New York City).

1769 – Chief Pontiac, chief of the Ottawa Indians, was murdered by an Illinois Indian, perhaps in retaliation for an earlier attack.

1777 - The first New York state constitution was formally adopted by the Convention of Representatives of the State of New York.

1792 - France declared war on Austria, Prussia and Sardinia in the War of the First Coalition.

1832 - Hot Springs Reservation was established by an act of Congress. Almost 90 years later, it would be called Hot Springs National Park.

1836 - The United States Congress separated the western part of Michigan Territory and formed a new territory to be known as Wisconsin.

1841 – "The Murders in the Rue Morgue," Edgar Allen Poe's first detective story, was published. The story, appearing in *Graham's Lady's and*

Gentleman's Magazine, featured C. Auguste Dupin, the first known fictional detective.

1862 – The first pasteurization test was completed by Louis Pasteur and Claude Bernard.

1871 – The Civil Rights Act of 1871 became law.

1906 - Firefighters finally began to control the fires in San Francisco after an earthquake two days earlier caused a substantial part of the city to burn.

1912 – This was opening day for baseball stadiums Tiger Stadium in Detroit, Michigan, and Fenway Park in Boston, Massachusetts.

1916 – The Chicago Cubs played their first game at Weeghman Park (currently Wrigley Field), defeating the Cincinnati Reds 7-6 in 11 innings.

1918 – Manfred von Richthofen, a.k.a. "The Red Baron," shot down his 79th and 80th victims marking his final victories before he was shot down and killed the following day.

1926 - Western Electric and Warner Bros. announce "Vitaphone," a process to add sound to film.

Manfred von Richthofen, the Red Baron from Willi Sanke's postcard #503. Public domain.

1945 - Allied bombers in Italy began a three-day attack on the bridges over the rivers Adige and Brenta to cut off German lines of retreat on the peninsula. Meanwhile, Adolf Hitler celebrated his 56th birthday as a Gestapo reign of terror resulted in the hanging of 20 Russian prisoners of war and 20 Jewish children; at least nine were under the age of 12.

1949 – Legendary jockey Willie Shoemaker won his first race riding a horse named "Shafter V" at Golden Gate Fields in Albany, California.

1961 – Fidel Castro announced that the Bay of Pigs invasion had been defeated.

1963 - The movie soundtrack album of *West Side Story* hit #1 on the pop LP chart and stayed there for two weeks.

1964 - Nelson Mandela delivered his "I Am Prepared to Die" speech at the opening of the Rivonia Trial, a classic of the anti-apartheid movement.

1968 - Pierre Trudeau became Canada's 15th Prime Minister.

1979 – President Jimmy Carter was attacked by a "swamp rabbit" while fishing in his hometown of Plains, Georgia.

Jimmy Carter confronting a "swamp rabbit." The original image was provided courtesy of The Jimmy Carter Library. Public domain.

1985 - The British pop music group Wham!, with singer George Michael, became the first group to release cassettes in the People's Republic of China, and those cassettes were given free to people who bought tickets to their concert in Hong Kong. Until then, the sale of Western pop products in China was illegal.

1986 – Pianist Vladimir Horowitz performed in his native Russia for the first time in 61 years. He had immigrated in 1925.

1986 – Basketball player Michael Jordan set the all-time record for points in an NBA playoff game with 63 against the Boston Celtics.

1989 - NATO debated modernizing short-range missiles; although the U.S. and UK agreed, West German Chancellor Helmut Kohl obtained a concession thus deferring a decision.

1992 - *The Freddie Mercury Tribute Concert*, held at Wembley Stadium, was televised live to over 1-billion people and raised millions of dollars for AIDS research.

1992 - British comedian Benny Hill died from heart problems in his home in England at age 68.

1998 – TAME Boeing 727-200 chartered by Air France crashed into Cerro El Cable Mountain after takeoff from Bogotá, Colombia, killing all 53 on board. The cause of the accident was determined to be a combination of bad weather and human error: the crew failed to execute the proper departure procedure immediately after takeoff, instead continuing in a straight line until impacting the hill.

1998 – German terrorist group Red Army Faction announces their dissolution after 28 years.

1999 – Students Eric Harris and Dylan Klebold killed 13 people and injured 24 others before committing suicide at Columbine High School in Jefferson County, Colorado.

Harris and Klebold at Columbine High School after killing 13 people, and injuring several more. Both students later commited suicide. Photo is from a stream of Columbine High School closed circuit television. Public domain.

2007 – A man with a handgun barricaded himself in NASA's Johnson Space Center in Houston, Texas before killing a male hostage and himself.

2008 – Danica Patrick wins the Indy Japan 300, becoming the first female driver in history to win an Indy car race.

2010 – The Deepwater Horizon oil platform exploded in the Gulf of Mexico, killing eleven workers. The resulting oil spill, one of the largest in history, spread for several months damaging the waters and the United States coastline, and prompting international debate and doubt about the practice and procedures of offshore drilling.

APRIL 21ST

BIRTHDAYS FOR APRIL 21ST

1782 Friedrich Fröbel; German educator and author, toymaker

1816 Charlotte Bronte; author

1838 John Muir; conservationist

1915 Anthony Quinn; Academy Award-winning actor

1924 Don Cornell; singer

1924 Ira Louvin; Country music singer, songwriter, and musician

1924 Clara Ward; singer

1926 Queen Elizabeth II (Elisabeth Mary); Queen of the United Kingdom

1930 Silvana Mangano; actress

1932 Elaine May; actress, comedienne, director

1935 Charles Grodin; actor

1936 Reg Fleming; hockey

1936 James Dobson; American evangelist

1940 Jacques Caron; hockey

1947 Al Bumbry; baseball

1947 Iggy Pop (James Newell Osterburg); singer, songwriter

1947 John Weider; musician, bassist

1948 Paul Davis; American singer

1949 Patti LuPone; actress

1951 Tony Danza; actor

1958 Andie MacDowell; actress

1959 Robert Smith; musician, guitarist, singer, songwriter

1963 John Cameron Mitchell; American film director

1969 Robin Meade; American news anchor

1970 Nicole Sullivan; American actress

2007 Princess Isabella of Denmark

EVENTS FOR APRIL 21ST

753 BC - According to tradition Romulus and his twin brother, Remus, found Rome on the site where they were suckled by a she-wolf as orphaned infants. Actually, the Romulus and Remus myth originated sometime in the fourth century B.C., and the exact date of Rome's founding was set by the Roman scholar Marcus Terentius Varro in the first century B.C.

1809 - Two Austrian army corps were driven from Landshut by a First French Empire army led by Napoleon I of France as two French corps to the north held off the main Austrian army on the first day of the Battle of Eckmühl.

1828 - *The American Dictionary of the English Language*, compiled by lexicographer and editor Noah Webster, was published.

1836 - The Mexicans were defeated by the Texans at the Battle of San Jacinto, thus ensuring Texan independence.

1856 - The first railroad bridge connecting Rock Island, Illinois and Davenport, Iowa over the Mississippi River opened with the first crossing of a locomotive.

1865 - A train carrying the coffin of assassinated President Abraham Lincoln left Washington, D.C. and headed towards Springfield, Illinois where he would be buried on May 4th.

1895 - In New York City, Woodville Latham demonstrated the first moving picture projected on a screen.

1910 – Writer Mark Twain (Samuel Langhorne Clemens) died at the age of 74 in Redding, Connecticut. Twain was once quoted as saying, "I came in with Halley's Comet in 1835. It is coming again next year, and I expect to go out with it. It will be the greatest disappointment of my life if I don't go out with Halley's Comet. The Almighty has said, no doubt: 'Now here are these two unaccountable freaks; they came in together, they must go out together.'" He died one day after the comet's closest approach to Earth.

Official portrait of Mark Twain in his DLitt (Doctor of Letters) academic dress, awarded by Oxford University. Public domain.

1940 - The debut of the CBS radio program *Take It or Leave It*; the show gave contestants the possibility of winning a top prize of $64.

1945 - Soviet Union forces south of Berlin, at Zossen, attacked the German High Command headquarters.

1951 - The National Olympic Committee of the Soviet Union was formed and participated in the Olympics the following year.

1956 - A 10-year-old "whiz kid" named Leonard Ross won $100,000 on the television quiz show *The Big Surprise* for his knowledge of the stock market. The following year he won the grand prize on *The $64,000 Challenge*. Ross, a child prodigy, graduated from high school at 14, finished college by 18, and went on to Yale Law School.

1956 - "Heartbreak Hotel" hit the top of the *Billboard* charts; Elvis' first number one hit.

1959 - Alf Dean caught the largest fish ever hooked by a rod and reel in South Australia. Alf's catch was a 16-foot, 10-inch white shark weighing 2,664 pounds!

The Seattle Space Needle shortly before the opening of the World's Fair. Public domain.

1962 – The Seattle World's Fair (Century 21 Exposition) opened, and was the first World's Fair in the United States since World War II.

1963 - The Beatles and The Rolling Stones meet for the first time at the Crawdaddy Club in

Richmond, England. Soon after, the Beatles gave the Stones "I Wanna Be Your Man" to record, and it became an early hit for the latter.

1965 – The New York World's Fair in Flushing Meadows reopened for it's second 6-month run.

1966 - Ian Brady and Myra Hindley went on trial at Chester Crown Court in England for the murders of 3 children who vanished between November 1963 and October 1965. Both were sentenced to life in prison.

Aerial view of the New York Worlds Fair Fairgrounds as it was still standing in 2004. Used by permission.

1967 - An outbreak of tornadoes plowed through the upper Midwest section of the United States (in particular the Chicago area, including the suburbs of Belvidere and Oak Lawn, Illinois, where 33 people were killed and 500 injured).

1968 - British Conservative politician Enoch Powell made his "rivers of blood" speech, warning of the dangers of immigration.

1969 - Yoshiaki Unetani, a Japanese marathon runner in a record field of 1,152 runners, won the Boston Marathon at a time of 2:13:49.

1970 - Sportscaster, Curt Gowdy was awarded the George Foster Peabody Award for achievement in radio and television.

1975 - South Vietnamese President Nguyen Van Thieu resigned after 10 years in office.

1977 - Annie, a musical based on Harold Gray's comic strip Little Orphan Annie, debuted at the Alvin Theatre on Broadway.

1980 - The Boston Marathon was disgraced when Rosie Ruiz, after having been proclaimed the winner, was proven to have not run the entire race.

1986 - Geraldo Rivera opened Al Capone's secret vault on *The Mystery of Al Capone's Vault*, discovering only a bottle of booze.

1989 - Tens of thousands of students and workers poured into Peking's Tiananmen Square in defiance of official warnings against anti-government protests.

1992 - California carried out its first execution in 25 years when double murderer Robert Alton Harris was put to death in the gas chamber. For his last words, he was quoted as saying, "You can be a king or a street sweeper, but everyone dances with the grim reaper."

1993 – The Supreme Court in La Paz, Bolivia, sentenced former dictator Luis Garcia Meza to 30 years in jail without parole for murder, theft, fraud and violating their constitution.

1994 – The first discoveries of planets outside of our solar system were announced by astronomer Alexander Wolszczan.

1996 - The center-left Olive Tree Coalition won the Italian general election, the left's first win since World War II.

1996 - Jimmy "the Greek" Snyder, age 76, died of heart failure in a Las Vegas hospital.

1997 – The ashes of 1960s LSD guru Timothy Leary and "Star Trek" creator Gene Roddenberry were blasted into space aboard a Pegasus XL rocket in the world's first space funeral.

Orbital Sciences' Lockheed L-1011 TriStar releasing a Pegasus rocket. Public domain.

2004 - Mordechai Vanunu, who revealed an Israeli nuclear weapons program in the 1980s, was released from prison in Israel after serving 18 years for treason.

APRIL 22nd

BIRTHDAYS FOR APRIL 22nd

1707 Henry Fielding; author

1870 Vladimir Ilyich Lenin; Russian premier

1904 Robert Oppenheimer; physicist

1906 Eddie Albert (Heimberger); actor

1923 Aaron Spelling; Emmy Award-winning executive producer

1926 Charlotte Rae; actress

1933 Mark Damon (Alan Harris); actor/director

1936 Glen Campbell; Grammy Award-winning singer

1937 Jack Nicholson; Academy Award-winning actor

1937 Jack Nitzsche; musician

1938 Deane Beman; golf

1939 Mel Carter; American singer

1939 Jason Miller; Pulitzer Prize winning playwright

1944 Steve Fossett; American adventurer

1946 John Waters; actor/director

1949 Spencer Haywood; basketball, U.S. Olympic gold medal

1950 Peter Frampton; musician, guitarist, singer

1951 Paul Carrack; English musician

1952 Marilyn Chambers; American pornographic actress

1953 Tom Lysiak; hockey

1954 Joseph Bottoms; actor

1959 Ryan Stiles; actor

1961 Byron Allen; comedian, TV host

1964 Chris Makepeace; actor

1983 Francis Capra; American actor

EVENTS FOR APRIL 22nd

1500 - Portuguese navigator Pedro Alvares Cabral, on a voyage to India, sailed far to the southwest and discovered Brazil, claiming it for Portugal.

1793 - President George Washington issued a Proclamation of Neutrality so the United States would not become involved in the war between France and Britain.

1838 – The British steamship *Sirius* became the first to cross the Atlantic from Britain to New York on steam power only.

The Cork Steam Ship Company's 700 ton, 320-horsepower *Sirius* built in 1837. Pubic domain.

1864 - The U.S. Congress passed the Coinage Act of 1864 mandating that the inscription "In God We Trust" be placed on all coins minted as United States currency.

1886 - Ohio passed a statute that made seduction unlawful. Covering all men over the age of 18 who worked as teachers or instructors of women, this law even prohibited men from having consensual sex with women (of any age) whom they were instructing. The penalty for disobeying this law ranged from two to 10 years in prison.

1889 – At high noon, thousands rushed to claim land in the Land Run of 1889. Within hours the cities of Oklahoma City and Guthrie were formed with populations of at least 10,000.

1906 – The 1906 Summer Olympics, not yet recognized as part of the official Olympic games, opened in Athens. France won fifteen Gold Medals, the USA was second with twelve, and Greece came in third with eight. (Note: the International Olympic Committee no longer recognizes these medals.)

1914 - Babe Ruth made his professional baseball-pitching debut while playing for the Baltimore Orioles. On that day Baltimore handily defeated the Buffalo Bison 6-0.

1915 – The use of poison gas in World War I escalated when chlorine gas was released as a chemical weapon in the Second Battle of Ypres.

1944 - Allied forces landed on Dutch New Guinea at Hollandia in World War II.

1945 – After learning that Soviet forces had taken Eberswalde without a fight, Adolf Hitler admitted defeat in his underground bunker and stated that suicide was his only recourse.

1954 – Senator Joseph McCarthy began hearings investigating the United States Army for being "soft" on Communism.

1956 - Elvis Presley flew west where he would make his Las Vegas debut the following day.

1961 - Four French generals who opposed De Gaulle's policies in Algeria failed in a coup attempt.

1969 - British lone yachtsman Robin Knox-Johnston arrived at Falmouth after completing the first solo nonstop circumnavigation of the Earth in just 312 days.

1970 - Henry Ross Perot, a future United States Presidential candidate, reportedly lost $450 million in the stock market.

1970 - The first Earth Day was observed. Using the slogan "Give Earth a Chance," Earth Day is celebrated on either this anniversary or on the vernal equinox.

1972 – Increased American bombing in Vietnam prompted anti-war protests in Los Angeles, New York City, and San Francisco.

1972 – Sylvia Cook and John Fairfax finished rowing across the Pacific. They departed from San Francisco and arrived at Hayman Island in Australia almost one year later. Why? We may never know.

1975 - Honduran President General Osvaldo Lopez Arellano was overthrown in a bloodless coup and replaced by Gen. Juan Alberto Melgar Castro.

1976 – ABC News announced that Barbara Walters would become the first anchorwoman of an evening network news program. Her national news debut would be made the following October.

1977 – Optical fiber was first used to carry live telephone traffic.

1978 - It was Marshall Checker, of the legendary Checker brothers, who first discovered them in the blues clubs of Chicago's South Side in 1969 and handed them their big break nine years later with an introduction to music-industry heavyweight and host of television's *Rock Concert*, Don Kirshner. Actually, none of that is true, but it's the story that *Saturday Night Live's* Paul Shaffer told as he announced the television debut of that night's musical guest, the Blues Brothers, the musical creation of *SNL* cast members Dan Aykroyd and John Belushi.

1979 – The Albert Einstein Memorial was unveiled at The National Academy of Sciences in Washington, D.C. on Constitution Avenue.

1983 - Australia expelled the First Secretary of the Soviet Embassy, Valery Ivanov, under suspicions of being a spy.

1983 – The German magazine Der Stern claimed that the "Hitler Diaries" had been found in wreckage in East Germany; the diaries were subsequently revealed to be forgeries.

A portrait of photographer Ansel Adams, which first appeared in the 1950 Yosemite Field School yearbook. Public domain.

1984 – Photography legend Ansel Adams died in Carmel, California, at age 82.

1983 – Reactor shutdown due to failure of fuel rods occurred at the Kursk Nuclear Power Plant, Russia.

1985 - Washington and Lee University researchers said that the first husband of Martha Dandrige Custis Washington left her $29,650 in Colonial

Virginia currency (the equivalent of $5.9 million today) before she married George.

1990 - A United States hostage in Lebanon, Robert Polhill, was released; he had been held since January 24, 1987.

1992 - A series of underground gas explosions tore apart a working-class neighborhood in the Mexican city of Guadalajara, killing some 200 people and about 15,000 were left homeless.

1994 - Former United States president Richard Nixon died at age 81 following complications of a massive stroke. He was the only President to resign the office as well as the only person to be elected twice to both the Presidency and the Vice Presidency.

1993 – The Holocaust Memorial Museum in Washington, D.C. was dedicated by President Bill Clinton. The museum opened to the public four days

Interior of the United States Holocaust Memorial Museum, located south of the National Mall, on 14th Street, S.W., in Washington, D.C. Used by permission.

later, and its first visitor was the 14th Dalai Lama of Tibet.

1996 – After Irma Bombeck had been diagnosed with polycystic kidney disease she was taken to a San Francisco hospital for a kidney transplant which was performed on April 3rd. However, she suffered complications following the procedure and died on this date at age 69.

1997 – A 126-day hostage crisis at the residence of the Japanese ambassador in Lima, Peru ended after government commandos stormed and captured the building, rescuing 71 hostages. One hostage died of a heart attack, 2 soldiers were killed by rebel fire, and all 14 Tupac Amaru rebels were slain.

1998 – Disney's Animal Kingdom opened at Walt Disney World near Orlando, Florida, United States.

The Expedition Everest roller coaster attraction at Disney's Animal Kingdom theme park in Florida. Photo by Benjamin D. Esham. Used by permission.

1998 - Autumn Jackson began serving a 26-month prison term for her attempted extortion of comedian Bill Cosby. Jackson claimed that Cosby was her father.

2000 – In a pre-dawn raid, federal agents seized six-year-old Elián González from his relatives' home in Miami, Florida.

2000 – Brazil officially celebrated its 500th anniversary with protests, especially from native and black populations.

2000 – The Big Number Change (an update of telephone dialing codes) took place in the United Kingdom. Virtually every phone number in the United Kingdom changed.

2000 – Second Battle of Elephant Pass: the Tamil Tigers launched this attack to capture this strategic Sri Lankan Army base. They captured it and held it for 8 years, creating the biggest military debacle in the history of the Sri Lankan military.

2004 – Two trains carrying explosives and fuel collided in Ryongchon, North Korea, killing 161 people, injuring 1,300 and destroying thousands of homes.

2006 – Over two hundred people were injured in a pro-democracy protest in Nepal after Nepali security forces opened fire on citizens protesting against King Gyanendra.

2008 – The United States Air Force retired the remaining F-117 Nighthawk aircraft in service.

2008 – Surgeons at London's Moorfields Eye Hospital performed the first operations using bionic eyes, implanting them into 2 blind patients.

2010 – Deepwater Horizon, an oil rig owned by BP and Transocean, sank to the bottom of the Gulf Of Mexico after having a blowout two days earlier. The well then created the largest oil spill to date by constantly gushing oil through the damaged wellhead for three straight months.

APRIL 23rd

BIRTHDAYS FOR APRIL 23rd

1564 William Shakespeare; poet, playwright

1621 William Penn; English admiral

1791 James Buchanan; 15th U.S. President

1813 Stephen Douglas; politician

1856 Granville T. Woods; inventor

1858 Max Planck; formulator of quantum theory of physics

1928 Shirley Temple Black; child actress, former ambassador to Ghana, TV hostess

1930 Alan Oppenheimer; actor

1932 Halston (Roy Frowick); fashion designer

1936 Roy Orbison; singer

1937 Don Massengale; golf

1939 Ray Peterson; singer

1939 Lee Majors (Harvey Lee Yeary II); actor

1941 David Birney; actor

1942 Sandra Dee (Alexandra Zuck); actress

1943 Herve Villechaize; actor

1943 Tony Esposito; Hockey Hall of Famer

1944 Marty Fleckman; golf

1947 Bernadette Devlin; Irish civil rights leader

1949 Joyce DeWitt; actress

1952 Narada Michael Walden; musician, drummer

1954 Michael Moore; American filmmaker

1955 Captain Sensible (Ray Burns); musician, singer

1955 Judy Davis; actress

1957 Jan Hooks; actress

1960 Valerie Bertinelli; actress

1960 Steve Clark; musician, guitarist

1961 Terry Gordy; American professional wrestler

1961 George Lopez; American actor and comedian

1968 Timothy McVeigh; American terrorist

1977 John Cena; American professional wrestler

EVENTS FOR APRIL 23rd

1564 - The birth of William Shakespeare, England's greatest playwright, is traditionally celebrated on this date. He died on the same date in 1616.

John Shakespeare's house, believed to be Shakespeare's birthplace, in Stratford-upon-Avon. Photo used by permission.

1597 – William Shakespeare's *The Merry Wives of Windsor* was first performed, with Queen Elizabeth I in attendance.

1616 - Spanish writer Miguel de Cervantes, creator of the knight-errant *Don Quixote de la Mancha*, died at age 68.

1633 - The League of Heilbronn was established; it united South German Protestants with Sweden and France against the Catholic League and the Imperialists.

1635 – The first public school in the United States, Boston Latin School, was founded in Boston, Massachusetts.

1661 - Charles II was crowned king of England in Westminster Abbey.

1789 - President-elect George Washington and his wife moved into the first executive mansion, the Franklin House, in New York.

1789 - *Courier De Boston* was first published in Boston, Massachusetts, making it the first newspaper in the United States to be published entirely in French.

Poster advertising Edison's Vitascope. Circa 1896. Public domain.

1896 – The new Edison "Vitascope" movie projector was publicly demonstrated for the first time at Koster and Bial's Music Hall, in New York City.

1900 - The word "hillbilly" was first printed in an article in the *New York Journal*; it was spelled, "Hill-Billie."

1940 - About 200 people died in a dance hall fire in Natchez, Mississippi. As windows had been boarded up in the Rhythm Club to prevent outsiders from viewing or listening to the music, the crowd was trapped. More than 300 people struggled to get out after the blaze began. A handful of people were able to get out the front door or through the ticket booth, while the remainder tried to press their way to the back door.

1941 - King George of the Hellenes and the Greek government fled the Greek mainland from the advancing Germans; the Greek army also surrendered.

1954 - Hank Aaron, playing for the Milwaukee Braves, hit his first major-league baseball home run.

1956 - Elvis made his first appearance in Las Vegas. The audience, mostly middle-aged, was so unimpressed with the rock and roll star that his two-week run was cancelled after only a week.

1961 – Judy Garland performed a legendary comeback concert at Carnegie Hall in New York City. The resulting two-album set *Judy* at Carnegie Hall was certified gold, charting for 95 weeks on *Billboard*, including 13 weeks at #1. The album won four Grammy Awards including "Album of the Year" and "Best Female Vocal of the Year."

1967 – Soyuz 1 was a Soviet manned spaceflight carrying cosmonaut Colonel Vladimir Komarov. Komarov was killed when the spacecraft crashed during its return to Earth, making his death the first confirmed in-flight

Official Soviet stamp honoring Vladimir Komarov. Public domain.

fatality in the history of spaceflight.

1968 - The United Methodist Church was created by the union of the former Methodist and Evangelical United Brethren churches.

1968 - Surgeons at the Hôpital de la Pitié, Paris, performed Europe's first heart transplant, on Clovis Roblain.

1968 – Students protesting against the Vietnam War in New York City took over administration buildings of Columbia University and shut down the university.

1969 - Sirhan Sirhan was sentenced to death in the gas chamber for assassinating New York Sen. Robert F. Kennedy. The sentence was later reduced to life imprisonment.

1983 – Olympian athlete and star of the silver screen, Buster Crabbe, died from a heart attack at age 75.

1985 - The Coca-Cola Company of Atlanta, Georgia, announced it was changing

 its 99-year-old secret formula and made what was considered by some to be the marketing blunder of all time. The original formula was back on the market in less than 3 months.

Pink Floyd playing *Dark Side of the Moon* at Earls Court, 1973. Photo by Tim Duncan. Used by permission.

1988 – Pink Floyd's album *Dark Side of the Moon* left the charts for the first time after spending a record of 741 consecutive weeks (over 14 years) on the *Billboard 200*.

1987 – Twenty-eight construction workers died when the L'Ambiance Plaza apartment building collapsed while under construction in Bridgeport, Connecticut.

1992 - McDonalds opened its first fast-food restaurant in the Chinese capital of Beijing. (Serving over 40,000 customers on its first day, this was also the biggest McDonalds in the world.)

1996 - Former Australian Labor Prime Minister Paul Keating resigned from parliament, ending a political career of 27 years.

1996 - A Bronx civil-court jury ordered Bernhard Goetz to pay $43 million to paralyzed Darrell Cabey, one of four young men he shot on a subway car in 1984.

1996 - A three-night auction of the late Jacqueline Kennedy Onassis' possessions began at Sotheby's in New York with a bidding frenzy.

1997 – The largest Omaria massacre took place in the Algerian village of Omaria near Médéa, south of Algiers. Attackers armed with knives, sabers, and guns killed 42 people (including 17 women and 3 babies) in 3 hours.

2003 – Beijing closed all of its schools for two weeks because of the SARS virus.

2009 – The gamma ray burst GRB 090423 was observed for 10 seconds as the most distant object of any kind, and also the oldest known object in the universe.

APRIL 24th

BIRTHDAYS FOR APRIL 24th

1743 Edmund Cartwright; inventor

1916 Lou Thesz; American professional wrestler

1934 Shirley MacLaine (Beaty); Academy Award-winning actress

1936 Jill Ireland; actress

1937 Joe Henderson; musician, composer

1940 Sue Grafton; author

1942 Richard M. Daley; Mayor of Chicago

1942 Barbra Joan Streisand; Grammy Award-winning singer, actress, director

1943 Richard Sterban; musician, bassist, singer

1944 Bill Singer; baseball

1944 Jim Geringer; 30th Governor of Wyoming

1945 Doug Clifford; musician, drummer

1945 Bob Lunn; golf

1947 Glenn Cornick; musician, bassist

1948 A. Paul Cellucci; 69th Governor of Massachusetts

1953 Eric Bogosian; actor

1954 Vince Ferragamo; football

1955 Michael O'Keefe; actor

1963 Billy Gould; musician, bassist

1964 Cedric the Entertainer (Cedric Antonio Kyles); American comedian and actor

1972 Chipper Jones; baseball

1976 George Prescott Bush; Son of Florida Governor Jeb Bush

1978 Eric Balfour; actor, musician

1980 Danny Gokey; American singer

1982 Kelly Clarkson; American singer

EVENTS FOR APRIL 24th

1558 - Mary Queen of Scots, aged 16, married the dauphin of France, the future Francois II.

1704 - The first regular newspaper in the United States, the *News-Letter*, was published in Boston, Massachusetts.

1800 – The United States Library of Congress was established when President John Adams signed legislation to appropriate $5,000 to purchase "such books as may be necessary for the use of Congress."

1833 – Jacob Ebert and George Dulty patented the soda fountain.

Construction of the Thomas Jefferson Building of the US Library of Congress from July 8, 1888 to May 15, 1894.
Public domain.

1907 – Hersheypark, founded by Milton S. Hershey, was opened originally for the exclusive use of his employees.

1913 – The Woolworth Building skyscraper in New York City was opened to the general public and was the world's tallest building until 1930.

The Woolworth Building under construction, circa 1912. Public domain.

1945 - American forces continued the liberation of the Dachau concentration camp.

1950 - Jordan formally annexed the West Bank and East Jerusalem, giving all residents automatic Jordanian citizenship. West Bank residents had already received the right to claim Jordanian citizenship in December 1949.

1953 - Queen Elizabeth II knighted Winston Churchill, the British leader who guided Great Britain and the Allies through the crisis of World War II.

1957 – The Suez Canal was reopened following the introduction of UNEF peacekeepers to the region.

1961 – The 17th century Swedish ship *Vasa* was salvaged in a busy shipping lane just outside Stockholm almost entirely intact. The boat had been built top-heavy and sank during its maiden voyage in 1628. The ship now rests in the *Vasa* Museum in Stockholm and as of this writing was one of Sweden's most popular tourist attractions.

Vasa's **port bow. Photo by Javier Kohen. Used by permission.**

1961 - Los Angeles Dodger, Sandy Koufax, struck out 18 batters in a game, making him the first major-league pitcher to do so on two separate occasions (the first time was August 31st, 1959).

1969 - The singing family, The Cowsills, got a gold record for their single, "Hair," from the same titled Broadway show. (Incidentally, in 1969 Screen Gems approached the family to portray themselves in their own TV sitcom, but when they were told that their mother was to be replaced by actress Shirley

Jones the deal fell through. Screen Gems later hired David Cassidy to join the cast and the show went on to be called *The Partridge Family*.)

1967 – American General William Westmoreland said in a news conference that the enemy had "gained support in the United States that gives him hope that he can win politically that which he cannot win militarily."

1970 - The Gambia was proclaimed a republic within the British Commonwealth.

1971 - A tsunami over 250 feet high rose over the Ryukyu Islands in Japan. The wave was so powerful it threw a 750-ton block of coral about 2.5 miles inland.

1970 – The first Chinese satellite, Dong Fang Hong I, was launched.

1974 - Bud Abbott died of cancer at age 76 in Woodland Hills, California.

1975 - Six Red Army Faction terrorists took over the West German embassy in Stockholm, took 11 hostages and demanded the release of the group's jailed members; shortly after, they were captured by Swedish police.

1980 – Eight U.S. servicemen died in "Operation Eagle Claw" as they attempted to end the Iran hostage crisis.

1980 - The 1980 Pennsylvania Lottery scandal, known as the "Triple Six Fix," was a plot to rig the Daily Number, a three-digit game the Pennsylvania Lottery offered. All of the balls except 4 and 6 were weighted, meaning that the drawing was almost sure to be a combination of only fours and sixes. The scheme was successful in that the number 666, an expected result, was drawn; however, the unusual betting patterns alerted authorities to the matter. The people who designed the scam eventually went to prison, and the winnings were never paid.

1982 – Jane Fonda extended her reach into the home-video market with the release of *Workout*, the first of her many bestselling aerobics tapes.

1983 – Manchester, Maine, schoolgirl Samantha Smith was invited to visit the Soviet Union by its leader Yuri Andropov, after he read her letter in which she expressed fears about nuclear war.

1990 – The Hubble Space Telescope was launched by the Space Shuttle *Discovery*.

The Hubble Telescope in orbit above the Earth. Photo take in 1990 from Space Shuttle *Atlantis*. Public domain.

1990 – Gruinard Island, Scotland, was officially declared free of the anthrax disease after 48 years of quarantine. The island was made dangerous for all mammals by experiments with the anthrax bacterium until its eventual decontamination.

1993 - The Provisional Irish Republican Army (IRA) detonated a truck bomb in London's financial district in Bishopsgate, City of London, England. One person was killed in the explosion and 44 were injured. Casualties were kept to a minimum due to the fact that a warning had been issued and much of the area had already been evacuated.

1995 - A United Nations tribunal named Bosnian Serb leader Radovan Karadzic and two of his senior aides as war crimes suspects.

1996 – Following the Oklahoma City Bombing, the United States government enacted the Antiterrorism and Effective Death Penalty Act of 1996.

1996 - Actress Margot Kidder was placed in a psychiatric ward after being found dirty, dazed, and fearful in a stranger's back yard in Glendale, California.

2004 – The United States lifted economic sanctions imposed on Libya 18 years earlier, as a reward for its cooperation in eliminating weapons of mass destruction.

2005 – Cardinal Joseph Ratzinger was inaugurated as the 265th Pope of the Roman Catholic Church, taking the name Pope Benedict XVI.

2005 – Snuppy, the world's first cloned dog, an Afghan, was born in South Korea.

2006 – King Gyanendra of Nepal gave into the demands of protesters and restored the parliament that he dissolved in 2002.

2007 – Iceland announced that Norway would shoulder the defense of Iceland during peacetime.

2007 – Gliese 581 c, a potentially habitable Earth-like extrasolar planet, was discovered in the constellation Libra.

2009 – The World Health Organization expressed concern considering the spread of influenza from Mexico and the United States to other countries. International cases and resulting deaths were confirmed.

APRIL 25th

BIRTHDAYS FOR APRIL 25th

1214 King Louis IX of France

1874 Guglielmo Marconi; inventor

1906 William J. Brennan, Jr.; U.S. Supreme Court Associate Justice

1908 Edward R. Murrow; newsman, Head of U.S. Information Agency

1917 Ella Fitzgerald; Grammy Award-winning singer

1923 Albert King; blues singer, musician, guitarist

1932 Meadowlark Lemon; basketball

1933 Jerry Leiber; record producer

1940 Al Pacino; Academy Award-winning actor

1942 Jon Kyl; U.S. Senator (AZ)

1945 Stu Cook; musician, bassist

1945 Bjorn Ulvaeus; musician, guitar, singer

1946 Talia Shire; actress

1947 Jeffrey De Munn; actor

1949 Michael Brown (Lookofsky); musician, keyboardist

1952 Don Martineau; hockey

1956 Dave Corzine; basketball

1964 Andy Bell; singer

1964 Hank Azaria; actor

1969 Renee Zellweger; actress

1976 Tim Duncan; basketball

EVENTS FOR APRIL 25th

1792 - Nicolas Jacques Pelletier became the first person to be guillotined in France, on the Place de Greve in Paris.

1831 - The New York and Harlem Railroad (one of the first railroads in the United States, and possibly also the world's first street railway) was incorporated.

1850 - Paul Julius Reuter, founder of the news agency that bears his name, used 40 pigeons to carry stock market prices between Brussels, Belgium, and Aachen, Germany; about 75 miles.

1859 - Ground was broken for the Suez Canal.

1862 - New Orleans fell to the Union fleet of Admiral David Farragut in the American Civil War.

1876 - The Chicago Cubs held their first National League game. Back then they were called the Chicago White Stockings and during that first game they shut out the Louisville Grays.

1898 - The United States declared war on Spain, and thus was the beginning of the Spanish-American War.

1901 - New York became the first state to require auto license plates.

1928 - Morris S. Frank was given the first seeing-eye dog (the dog's name was Buddy).

1944 – The United Negro College Fund was incorporated.

1952 – The American Bowling Congress approved the use of an automatic pinsetter.

Before the days of automatic pinsetters, the task was performed by young boys who often worked overnight. Photo circa 1910. Courtesy of the United States Library of Congress' Prints and Photographs division.

1953 – Francis Crick and James D. Watson published *Molecular Structure of Nucleic Acids*: a structure for deoxyribose nucleic acid describing the double helix structure of DNA.

1954 - Bell Laboratories announced the prototype of a new solar battery. Two demonstrations were given: the operation of a 21-inch Ferris wheel and the operation of a solar-powered radio transmitter.

1956 - Elvis Presley's "Heartbreak Hotel" went #1 and stayed in the top position for no less than eight weeks.

1959 - Mario Andretti made his racing debut driving his own 1948 Hudson to victory at the Nazareth Speedway in Nazareth, Pennsylvania.

1959 – The St. Lawrence Seaway, linking the North American Great Lakes and the Atlantic Ocean, officially opened to shipping.

1961 - Robert Noyce patented the integrated circuit, now referred to as a chip.

1961 – An unmanned Mercury test rocket exploded shortly after launch. The range safety officer terminated the mission after 43.3 seconds due to failure of the launch vehicle to follow its roll and pitch programs.

Example of the Mercury spacecraft launch escape system operation; this is not from the Mercury test flight and is shown here only for illustrative purposes. Public domain.

Although the launch vehicle was destroyed, considerable benefit was derived from the flight test. The launch escape system saved the Mercury spacecraft from destruction.

1964 - Thieves stole the head of the Little Mermaid statue in Copenhagen, Denmark (Henrik Bruun confessed in 1997). The head was never recovered and had to be reconstructed.

1965 – Teenage sniper Michael Andrew Clark killed three and wounded six others while shooting from a hilltop along Highway 101 just south of Santa Maria, California.

1967 - Colorado Governor John Arthur Love signed the first law legalizing abortion in the United States.

1974 - Dictator Antonio Salazar's regime was overthrown in Portugal four years after his death.

1975 - As North Vietnamese Army forces closed in on the South Vietnamese capital, the Australian Embassy was closed and evacuated, almost 10 years to the day since the first Australian troop commitment to South Vietnam.

1976 - Two protestors ran into the outfield of Dodger Stadium and tried to set fire to a U.S. flag. When Cubs outfielder Rick Monday noticed the flag on the ground and the men fumbling with matches and lighter fluid, he dashed over and snatched the flag to thunderous applause.

1978 - Queen's hit single "We Are the Champions" was certified platinum.

1978 - St. Paul, Minnesota, became the 2nd U.S. city to repeal its gay rights ordinance after Anita Bryant's successful 1977 anti-gay campaign in Dade County, Florida.

1982 – Israel completes its withdrawal from the Sinai Peninsula per the Camp David Accords.

1983 – Pioneer 10 traveled beyond Pluto's orbit and is currently on a path that will take it within the constellation Taurus in about 2-million years.

1985 - *Big River (The Adventures of Huckleberry Finn)* opened at the Eugene O'Neill Theatre on Broadway and ran for over 1,000 performances.

1989 - James Richardson walked out of a Florida prison 21 years after being wrongfully convicted of killing his seven children. In 1967, James and his wife, Annie, were working in a field picking fruit when Betsy Reese (their neighbor) came over to heat up a meal for the Richardsons' seven kids. After they finished eating, the children began foaming at the mouth and they were dead moments later from poisoning. James was convicted after Reese testified that she had seen that same kind of poison stored in a shed behind James' home. That same neighbor later admitted that it was she who committed the murders.

1989 – Motorola introduced the Motorola MicroTAC Personal Cellular Telephone; at the time it was the world's smallest mobile phone.

1990 - Violeta Chamorro was sworn in as president of Nicaragua having defeated Sandinista leader Daniel Ortega.

1994 - The largest high school arson ever in the United States was started at Burnsville High School, in Burnsville, Minnesota, resulting in over 15-million dollars in damages. Besides the irony of the name of the

A Motorola MicroTAC 9800X with Red LED display and it sold for a mere $2,495. Amazingly, the only thing this phone could do was make phone calls: no games, no texting, and no Internet. Public domain.

town, the school's nickname was "The Blaze;" all coincidences and unrelated to the arson. (The same arsonist also went on to set fires at Edina High School and Minnetonka High School.)

2002 - South African Mark Shuttleworth blasted off from the Baikonur Cosmodrome and became the second person in the world to be a paying passenger on a flight to space. He was launched aboard the Russian Soyuz TM-34 mission as a spaceflight participant, and paid approximately $20 million (US) for the voyage. After staying in the *International Space Station* for a week, he returned to Earth on May 5th.

The Obelisk of Axum in the Tigray Region back on home soil in Ethiopa. Photo by Ondřej Žváček. Used by permission.

2003 – The Human Genome Project came to an end 2.5 years before first anticipated.

2005 – The final piece of the Obelisk of Axum was returned to Ethiopia after being stolen by the invading Italian army in 1937.

2005 – Bulgaria and Romania signed accession treaties to join the European Union.

2005 – More than 100 people died in an Amagasaki rail crash in Japan.

2007 – Boris Yeltsin's funeral was the first to be sanctioned by the Russian Orthodox Church for a head of state since the funeral of Emperor Alexander III in 1894.

APRIL 26th

BIRTHDAYS FOR APRIL 26th

1785 John Audubon; ornithologist, artist

1812 Alfred Krupp; German industrialist

1822 Frederick Law Olmsted; American landscape architect, co-designer of New York's Central Park

1886 Ma Rainey; American singer

1894 Rudolf Hess; close friend, personal secretary to Hitler

1900 Charles Richter; seismologist

1910 Tomoyuki Tanaka; Japanese movie producer and creator of Godzilla

1917 Sal (Salvatore Anthony) Maglie; baseball

1918 Stafford Repp; American actor

1924 Teddy Edwards (Theodore Marcus); jazz musician, saxophonist

1926 Bambi Linn (Bambina Linnemeier); dancer, actress

1927 John Ralston; football, coach

1933 Carol Burnett; Emmy Award-winning entertainer

1937 Bob Boozer; basketball

1938 Nino Benvenuti; boxer

1938 Maurice Williams; singer, songwriter

1938 Duane Eddy; guitarist

1941 Claudine Clark; singer

1941 Gary Cuozzo; football

1941 Bruce MacGregor; hockey

1942 Bobby Rydell (Ridarelli); singer

1943 Gary Wright; musician

1947 Donna De Varona; Olympic Hall of Famer, swimming

1947 Amos (Joseph) Otis; baseball

1958 Giancarlo Esposito; actor

1960 Roger Taylor; British musician

1961 Joan Chen; actress

1962 Michael Damian; actor

1965 Kevin James; actor

1967 Kane (Glenn Jacobs); American professional wrestler

1983 Jessica Lynch; American P.O.W.

EVENTS FOR APRIL 26th

1865 – Union cavalry troopers cornered and shot dead John Wilkes Booth, President Lincoln's assassin, in Virginia.

1913 - Thirteen-year-old Mary Phagan was found sexually molested and murdered in the basement of the Atlanta, Georgia, pencil factory where she worked. Her murder later led to one of the most disgraceful episodes of bigotry, injustice, and mob violence in American history.

1915 - Italy secretly signed the Treaty of London with Britain, France, and Russia, which would put them on the side of the allies in World War I.

1921 - Weather broadcasts were heard for the first time at 10:05 am on radio when WEW in St. Louis, Missouri aired weather news.

1923 - The Duke of York (Britain's future King George VI) married Lady Elizabeth Bowes-Lyon in Westminster Abbey.

1925 – Paul von Hindenburg defeated Wilhelm Marx in the second round of the German presidential election and became the first directly-elected head of state

of the Weimar Republic and the 2nd President of the German Reich.

1931 - NBC radio presented *Lum and Abner*, which continued for 24 years.

1933 – The official secret police force of Nazi Germany, known formally as "the Gestapo," was established.

1937 - For the first and only time ever, *LIFE Magazine* was published without the word "LIFE" inside a red box in the

Paul v. Hindenburg, circa 1932. Photo courtesy of Deutsches Bundesarchiv (German Federal Archive). Used by permission.

upper left-hand corner. Instead, the magazine's logo appeared in a smaller format in the lower left-hand corner. A close-up of a Leghorn Rooster adorned the cover.

1942 - Over 1,500 miners were killed in a Chinese coalmine when a gas and coal-dust explosion ripped through the mineshaft.

1952 - Patty Berg set a record for the LPGA Richmond Golf Open when she shot a 64 over 18 holes at the tournament held in Richmond, California.

1954 - The Salk polio vaccine field trials, involving 1.8 million children, began at the Franklin Sherman Elementary School in McLean, Virginia.

1954 - Grace Kelly, "Hollywood's brightest and busiest star," was on *LIFE Magazine's* cover. Two years later she married Rainier III, Prince of Monaco, and became styled as Her Serene Highness The Princess of Monaco, and was commonly referred to as "Princess Grace."

1954 – The Geneva Conference, an effort to restore peace in Indochina and Korea, began.

1956 - Trucking entrepreneur Malcom McLean put 58 shipping containers aboard a refitted tanker ship, the *Ideal-X*, and sailed them from Newark to Houston.

Dining car menu from the Baltimore and Ohio Railroad's train, the *Royal Blue*. Public domain.

1958 – Today marked the final run of the Baltimore and Ohio Railroad's *Royal Blue* from Washington, D.C., to New York City. After 68 years, this was the first U.S. passenger train to use electric locomotives.

1962 – The Ranger 4 spacecraft crashed into the Moon. This spacecraft was the first U.S. spacecraft to reach another celestial body. Although it was planed to impact the lunar surface, a power failure in the central computer caused a crash a little earlier than expected.

1964 – Tanganyika and Zanzibar merged to form Tanzania.

1965 – A Rolling Stones concert in London, Ontario, was shut down by police after 15 minutes due to rioting.

1966 - A new government was formed in the Republic of Congo, led by Ambroise Noumazalaye.

1970 - Strip tease artist Gypsy Rose Lee died of lung cancer in Los Angeles, California, at the age of 59.

1975 - B.J. Thomas was in 1st place on *Billboard's* chart with the longest title to date ever for a number one song: "(Hey Won't You Play) Another Somebody Done Somebody Wrong Song."

1977 - A crowd began to gather outside of 254 West 54th Street in New York City to await the opening of what would become an icon of the disco craze: Studio 54.

1978 - Ringo Starr's, *Ringo*, a musical version of *The Prince and the Pauper*, aired on NBC. Ringo's fellow former Beatle, George Harrison, provided the narration.

1984 - President Ronald Reagan arrived in China for a diplomatic meeting with Chinese President Li Xiannian. This trip marked the first time a United States President had traveled to China since President Richard Nixon's historic trip in 1972.

1986 – A nuclear reactor accident occurred at the Chernobyl Nuclear Power Plant in the Soviet Union and created the world's worst nuclear disaster to date.

The infamous Reactor #4 from the Chernobyl power plant. This photo shows #4 completely enclosed in a concrete and lead sarcophagus to prevent further escape of radiation. Public domain.

1986 - Former Mr. Universe and international movie star Arnold Schwarzenegger, age 38, married news journalist Maria Shriver at St. Francis Xavier Roman Catholic Church.

1990 - Carlos Pizarro Leongomez, leader of the leftist Colombian guerrilla movement M-19 who gave up violence to run for president, was assassinated on a plane.

2002 – Nineteen-year old Robert Steinhäuser, an expelled student, infiltrated and killed 17 at Gutenberg-Gymnasium in Erfurt,Germany. He moved from classroom to classroom shooting anyone he could find. Altogether he killed 13 teachers and 2 students before he turned the gun on himself and committed suicide.

2005 – Under international pressure, Syria withdrew the last of its 14,000 troop military garrison in Lebanon, ending its 29-year military domination of that country.

2007 – Queen's Pier (named after Queen Victoria) was officially closed by the Hong Kong Government, after a bitter struggle by conservationists, in order to facilitate land reclamation in Hong Kong's Central district.

APRIL 27th

BIRTHDAYS FOR APRIL 27th

1791 Samuel F.B. (Finley Breese) Morse; inventor

1822 Ulysses Simpson Grant; 18th U.S. President

1899 Walter Lantz; Academy Award-winning animator

1922 Jack Klugman; Emmy Award-winning actor

1927 Coretta Scott King; civil rights leader

1932 Chuck Knox; football, coach

1932 Casey Kasem; radio, TV host

1933 Calvin Newborn; jazz/blues musician, guitarist

1934 Anouk Aimee; actress

1937 Sandy Dennis; Academy Award winning actress

1938 Bob Foster; Boxing Hall of Famer

1944 Cuba Gooding, Sr.; American musician (The Main Ingredient)

1944 Doug Buffone; football

1947 Pete Ham; musician, guitarist, singer

1947 Keith Magnuson; hockey

1948 Frank William Abagnale, Jr.; American con artist

1948 Kate Pierson; musician, organist, singer

1948 Clive Taylor; musician, bassist

1951 Paul (Ace) Frehley; musician

1952 George Gervin; basketball

1959 Sheena Easton (Sheena Shirley Orr); singer

1959 Marco Pirroni; musician, guitarist, songwriter

EVENTS FOR APRIL 27th

4977 BC - The universe was created, at least according to German mathematician and astronomer Johannes Kepler. Other scientists have since noted that Kepler's deduction was off by about 14 billion years.

1521 - Portuguese explorer Ferdinand Magellan died in battle when natives in the Philippines led by chief Lapu-Lapu killed him.

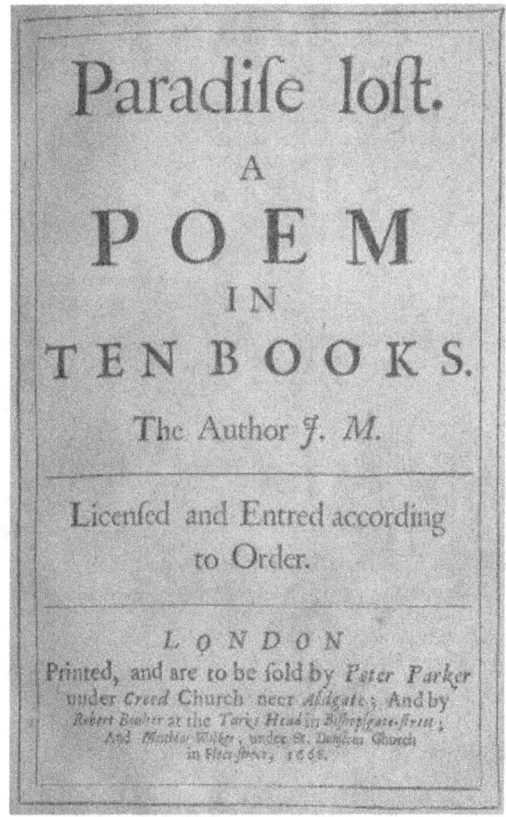

Title page of the first edition of John Milton's *Paradise Lost* from 1668. Public domain.

1667 – The blind and impoverished John Milton sold the copyright of *Paradise Lost* for £10 (about $15 USA).

1749 – Today marked the first performance of Handel's "Music for the Royal Fireworks" in Green Park, London. It was to celebrate the end of the War of the Austrian Succession and the signing of the Treaty of Aix-la-Chapelle in 1748.

1810 – Beethoven composed his famous piano piece, "Für Elise." This piece would not be published until more than 40 years after the composer's death.

1865 – The New York State Senate created Cornell University as the state's land grant institution.

View of Cornell Central Campus as it stands today. Public domain.

1865 – The steamboat *Sultana*, carrying 2,400 passengers, exploded and sank in the Mississippi River, killing 1,700, most of whom were Union survivors of the Andersonville and Cahaba Prisons.

Depiction of the *Sultana* disaster as it appeared in *Harpers Weekly*, May 20, 1865. Public domain.

1903 – The Jamaica Race Track opened in New York. Among those watching the horses run on the first day included Lillian Russell and Diamond Jim Brady.

1938 - Geraldine Apponyi became the first American woman to become a Queen when she married King Zog of Albania.

1938 – The first colored baseball was used in a baseball game. In a game between Columbia and Fordham Universities in New York City, a yellow ball was used. This fad, however, never caught on.

1941 - German tanks rolled into Athens in World War II.

1945 - German troops were finally expelled from Finnish Lapland and, at the same time, Italian partisans arrested Benito Mussolini, attempting escape disguised as a German soldier.

1947 - Organized baseball celebrated Babe Ruth Day at major-league parks in the United States and Japan where it was called "Babu Rusu Day."

1950 - The Group Areas Act was passed in South Africa, formally segregating the races. One effect of the law was to exclude non-Whites from living in the most developed areas, which were restricted to Whites (e.g., Sea Point). It also caused many non-Whites to have to commute large distances from their homes in order to be able to work.

1956 - Heavyweight boxing champion Rocky Marciano retired without losing a professional boxing match.

1960 - The submarine *Tullibee* launched from Groton, Connecticut and was the first to be equipped with the BQQ-2 Sonar system.

1960 – Togo gained independence from the French-administered UN trusteeship.

1961 - Sierra Leone gained independence within the Commonwealth from Great Britain, and parliament held its first session with Sir Milton Margai as prime minister.

1963 - Margaret Annemarie Battavio, better known as "Little Peggy March," hit #1 on the *Billboard* charts with "I Will Follow Him." In that she had just turned 15, she was the youngest person to date to hit the *Billboard Hot 100*.

1964 - John Lennon's book, *In His Own Write,* was published in the United States with an initial print run of 90,000 copies.

1967 – Expo 67 officially opened in Montreal, Canada, with a large opening ceremony broadcast around the world. It opened to the public the next day.

1972 - A no-confidence vote against German Chancellor Willy Brandt failed under obscure circumstances.

1974 – Ten thousand people marched in Washington, D.C., calling for the impeachment of US President Richard Nixon

1976 - Maxine Nightingale was awarded a gold record for the single, "Right Back Where We Started From."

1978 – Former United States President Nixon aide John D. Ehrlichman was released from an Arizona prison after serving 18 months for Watergate-related crimes.

1981 – Xerox PARC introduced a computer mouse that rolled on a single ball rather than external wheels.

1981 - Former Beatle Ringo Starr married Barbara Bach at the Marylebone Registry Office in London, England.

1986 - By overriding a Home Box Office broadcast, a video pirate, known only as "Captain Midnight," announced that he would not pay for his cable service.

Four about five minutes, people trying to watch *The Falcon and the Snowman*, saw a graphic which read "Good evening, HBO from Captain Midnight. $12.95 per month? No way! (Showtime/Movie Channel beware!)" Captain Midnight was later caught and identified as John R. MacDougall of Ocala, Florida. He received a $5,000 fine and one year's probation.

1987 – The United States Department of Justice declared incumbent Austrian president Kurt Waldheim an "undesirable alien."

Kurt Waldheim, the 9th president of Austria, and United Nations Secretary-General. Used by permission.

1992 – Betty Boothroyd became the first woman to be elected Speaker of the British House of Commons in its 700-year history.

1993 - A Zambian air force plane carrying Zambia's entire national soccer team crashed into the Atlantic off Gabon, killing all 30 aboard.

1994 – The first democratic general election was held in South Africa in which black citizens could vote.

2002 – The last successful telemetry from the NASA space probe Pioneer 10.

2002 - The Laughlin, Nevada, River Run Riot killed 3. Members of the Hell's Angels and the Mongols motorcycle clubs stabbed and shot at each other at Harrah's Laughlin. Mongol Anthony Barrera, 43, was stabbed to death, and two Hell's Angels, Jeramie Bell, 27, and Robert Tumelty, 50, were shot to death.

2005 – The Superjumbo jet aircraft Airbus A380 made its first flight from Toulouse, France.

2006 – Construction began on the Freedom Tower for the new World Trade Center in New York City. As of March 30, 2009, the Port Authority said that the building will be known officially as "One World Trade Center."

2007 – Estonian authorities removed the Bronze Soldier, a Soviet Red Army war memorial in Tallinn, amid political controversy with Russia.

The progress of 1-WTC from West Street as of February 2011. Photo by Jason Andrew Layne. Used by permission.

APRIL 28th

BIRTHDAYS FOR APRIL 28th

1758 James Monroe; 5th U.S. President

1878 Lionel Barrymore; Academy Award-winning actor

1908 Oskar Schindler; Austrian businessman

1911 Lee Falk; American comic strip writer

1928 Eugene M. Shoemaker; American planetary scientist

1941 Ann-Margret (Olsson); actress

1945 John Wolters; musician, drummer

1948 Marcia Strassman; actress

1948 Pablo Torrealba; baseball

1949 Bruno Kirby; actor

1950 Jay Leno; comedian, TV talk show host

1950 Jim Wiley; hockey

1953 Tony Peters; football

1964 Barry Larkin; baseball

1966 John Daly; golfer

1971 Chris Young; actor

1981 Jessica Alba; actress

EVENTS FOR APRIL 28th

1788 - Maryland became the 7th state to ratify the Constitution of the United States.

1789 – A rebel crew took control of the British ship HMS *Bounty*, leaving the ship's leader, Lieutenant William Bligh, and his supporters adrift in the South Pacific Ocean.

The mutineers turning Lt Bligh and part of the officers and crew adrift from HMAV *Bounty*. Painting by Robert Dodd. Public domain.

1792 – France invaded the Austrian Netherlands (Belgium, as its known today), and thus began the French Revolutionary War.

1896 – Joseph Smith Duncan of Sioux City, Indiana, was granted patent #558,936 for the Addressograph.

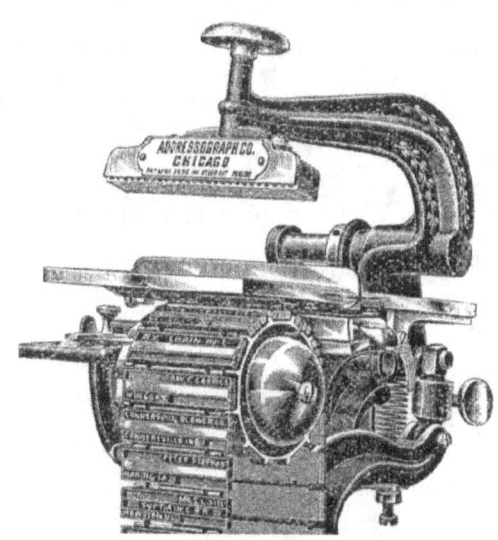

Illustration of 1896 Addressograph with movable belt of rubber plates. And thus the era of junk mail began. Public domain.

1902 – Using the ISO 8601 standard Year Zero definition for the Gregorian calendar preceded by the Julian calendar, the one-billionth minute since the start of January 1, Year Zero occurred at 10:40 AM.

1930 – The first night game in organized baseball history took place in Independence, Kansas.

1932 - A vaccine to fight yellow fever in humans was announced.

1940 - Glenn Miller recorded "Pennsylvania 6-5000." (By the way, this is, and was, a real phone number for the Hotel Pennsylvania and is believed to be the oldest continuing phone number in New York City.)

1945 – Italian dictator Benito Mussolini and his mistress were executed by firing squad near Lake Como one day after his capture.

1947 – Thor Heyerdahl and five crew mates set out from Peru on the *Kon-Tiki* to prove that Peruvian natives could have settled Polynesia.

The *Kon Tiki* which sailed across the Pacific Ocean from South America to the Polynesian islands, some 4,300 miles. The trip took 101 days. Public domain.

1952 – Dwight D. Eisenhower resigned as Supreme Allied Commander of NATO.

1952 - The Treaty of San Francisco went into effect, formally ending the war between Japan and the Allies, and simultaneously ending the occupation of the four main Japanese islands. The treaty was signed at the War Memorial Opera House in San Francisco, California.

1957 - Mike Wallace was seen nation-wide for the first time as the host of *The Mike Wallace Interview*.

1962 - Jim Grelle became the fourth American runner to break the four-minute mile with a mark of 3 minutes, 59.9 seconds.

1965 - U.S. troops were sent to the Dominican Republic by President Lyndon B. Johnson, "for the stated purpose of protecting U.S. citizens and preventing an alleged Communist takeover of the country," thus thwarting the possibility of "another Cuba."

1967 - Muhammad Ali (a.k.a. Cassius Clay) refused to join the United States Army. During his induction he refused three times to step forward at the call of his name. An officer warned him he was committing a felony punishable by five years in prison and a fine of $10,000. Once more, Ali refused to budge when his name was called. As a result, he was arrested and on the same day the New York State Athletic Commission suspended his boxing license and stripped him of his title.

1969 - Charles de Gaulle steps down as president of France after suffering defeat in a referendum the day before.

1970 – U.S. President Richard M. Nixon formally authorized American combat troops to fight communist sanctuaries in Cambodia.

1973 - Six Irishmen, including Joe Cahill, were arrested by the Irish Naval Service off County Waterford, on board a coaster carrying 5 tons of weapons destined for the Provisional Irish Republican Army.

1985 - The largest sand castle in the world to date was completed, at a height of four stories tall near St. Petersburg, Florida.

1985 - Parker, Texas saw a 2-to-1 rise in the ratio of tourists to residents; travelers flocked to see Southfork Ranch of CBS-TV's, *Dallas*.

1988 – Flight attendant Clarabelle "C.B." Lansing was blown from Aloha Airlines Flight 243, a Boeing 737, and fell 24,000 feet to her death when part of the plane's fuselage ripped open in mid-flight. The accident was later blamed on metal fatigue.

1990 – After 6,137 performances, *A Chorus Line* closed on Broadway.

1996 - Martin Bryant shot and killed 35 people when he ran amok in the tourist area of Port Arthur in Tasmania.

1996 – President Bill Clinton delivered a 4½ hour videotaped testimony for the defense during the Whitewater controversy.

1999 - Rory Calhoun, leading actor in many Westerns, died from complications resulting from emphysema and diabetes in Burbank, California. Calhoun was 76.

2001 – Millionaire Dennis Tito became the world's first space tourist when he spent $20 million to stay for a week aboard the International Space Station.

2004 – Abu Ghraib prisoner abuse in Iraq was revealed on the television show *60 Minutes II* (later re-named *60 Minutes Wednesday*).

2004 – Comcast, America's largest cable operator, was in the process of taking over the Walt Disney Corporation in a hostile takeover bid of $54 billion. Disney, however, refused to entertain the proposal and Comcast backed away from the deal.

2005 – The Patent Law Treaty went into effect and created uniformity in the patent process between 59 nations. As of this writing, the United States was not a part of this treaty.

APRIL 29th

BIRTHDAYS FOR APRIL 29th

1745 Oliver Ellsworth; 3rd U.S. Supreme Court Chief Justice

1863 William Randolph Hearst; publisher

1899 Duke (Edward Kennedy) Ellington; musician

1901 Hirohito; Emperor of Japan

1933 Rod McKuen; poet and composer

1934 Luis Aparicio; Baseball Hall of Famer

1936 Zubin Mehta; conductor

1936 April Stevens (Carol Lo Tempio); singer

1937 Jean Gauthier; hockey

1938 Bernard Madoff; American convict, Ponzi scheme operator

1943 Duane Allen; singer

1944 Jim Hart; football

1947 Jim Ryun; runner

1947 Tommy James; singer

1947 Johnny Miller; golf

1950 Phillip Noyce; Australian film director

1951 Dale Earnhardt; Champion Nascar driver

1952 Nora Dunn; actress

1954 Jerry Seinfeld; Emmy Award-winning comedian, actor

1955 Kate Mulgrew; actress

1957 Daniel Day-Lewis; Academy Award-winning actor

1958 Michelle Pfeiffer; actress

1958 Eve Plumb; actress

1968 Carnie Wilson; singer

1970 Andre Agassi; tennis

1970 Uma Thurman; actress

EVENTS FOR APRIL 29th

1429 - Joan of Arc entered Orleans with supplies seven months into the siege of the city in the Hundred Years War.

1879 - Electric arc lights were used for the first time (Cleveland, Ohio).

1882 – The "Elektromote," the forerunner of the trolleybus, was tested by Ernst Werner von Siemens in Berlin.

1916 - The British 6th Indian Division surrenders to Ottoman Forces at the Siege of Kut in one of the largest surrenders of British forces up to that point.

1945 – Adolf Hitler married his long-time partner Eva Braun in a Berlin bunker and designated Admiral Karl Dönitz as his successor. The honeymoon was short, however; the newlyweds committed suicide the following day.

1945 - The 522nd Field Artillery Battalion freed the remaining prisoners of the Nazi death camp, Dachau.

1945 - The terms of surrender of the German armies in Italy were signed.

1946 – "Father Divine," a controversial religious leader who claimed to be God, married the much-younger Edna Rose Ritchings (he was 70, she was 21), a celebrated anniversary in the International Peace Mission movement.

1953 – The first U.S. experimental 3D-TV broadcast showed an episode of *Space Patrol* on Los Angeles ABC affiliate KECA-TV.

1961 - *ABC's Wide World of Sports* made its television debut.

1963 - Buddy Rogers became the first WWF Champion.

President Richard M. Nixon presenting the Presidential Medal of Freedom to Duke Ellington. Photo courtesy of the National Archives.

1968 – The controversial musical *Hair* opened on Broadway.

1969 – On his 70th birthday Sir Duke, Duke Ellington, was presented with the Medal of Freedom, the United States government's highest civilian honor.

1974 - Phil Donahue's television show, *Donahue*, moved from Dayton, Ohio, to Chicago, Illinois.

1974 - President Richard Nixon announced to the public that he would release transcripts of 46 taped White House conversations in response to a Watergate trial subpoena issued in July 1973.

1975 - In the closing hours of the Vietnam War, the last United States troops were evacuated from Saigon.

1980 – The master of horror/suspense films, director Alfred Hitchcock died in his sleep from natural causes at age 80.

1981 - Steve Carlton, pitcher for the Philadelphia Phillies, became the first left-handed person in the major leagues to obtain 3,000 career strikeouts when he struck out Tim Walloch of the Expos.

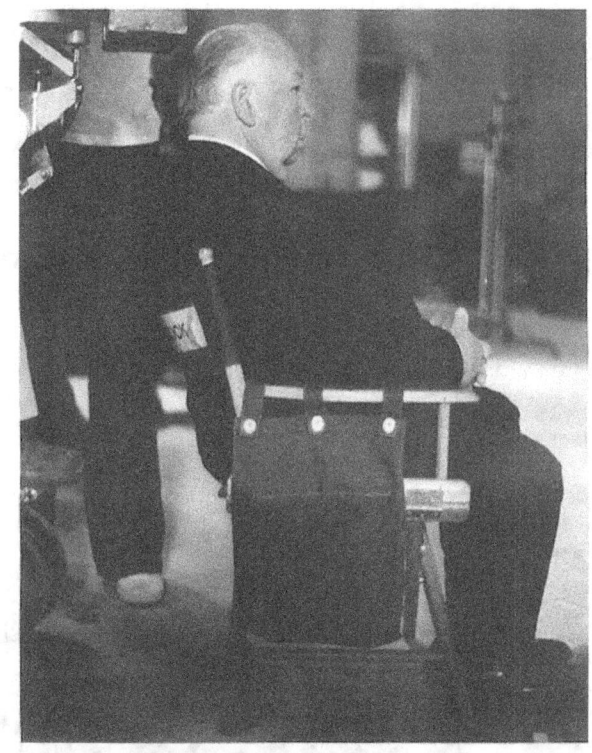

Alfred Hitchcock directing Family Plot inside Grace Cathedral, San Francisco, California. Photo by Stan Osborne. Used by permission.

1981 - In England, Peter Sutcliffe admitted he was the Yorkshire Ripper, murderer of 13 women.

1985 - George Steinbrenner, owner of the New York Yankees, fired manager Yogi Berra 16 games into the baseball season.

1986 – Boston Red Sox pitcher Roger Clemens set a Major League Baseball record with 20 strikeouts in nine innings against the Seattle Mariners.

1986 – An arson fire at the Central library of the City of Los Angeles Public Library destroyed 400,000 books and other items.

1992 - A jury acquitted four Los Angeles, California, police officers accused of beating motorist Rodney King. The verdict sparked three days of rioting and looting during which 53 people lost their lives.

1994 – Commodore International, the maker of Commodore Computers, declared bankruptcy.

1997 – The Chemical Weapons Convention of 1993 went into force; it outlawed the production, stockpiling and use of chemical weapons among its signatories.

2002 – The United States was re-elected to the United Nations Commission on Human Rights, one year after losing the seat it had held for 50 years.

2004 – Dick Cheney and George W. Bush testified before the 9/11 Commission in a closed, unrecorded hearing in the Oval Office.

2004 – Oldsmobile built its final car ending 107 years of production.

2004 - The National World War II Memorial in Washington, D.C., opened to thousands of visitors, providing overdue recognition for the 16 million U.S. men and women who served in the war.

2005 – Syria completed withdrawal from Lebanon, ending 29 years of occupation.

APRIL 30th

BIRTHDAYS FOR APRIL 30th

1662 Queen Mary II of England

1908 Eve Arden; American actress

1923 Al Lewis; American actor

1925 Johnny Horton; American musician

1926 Cloris Leachman; Academy Award-winning actress

1933 Willie Nelson; singer

1938 Gary Collins; actor

1940 Burt Young; actor

1941 Johnny Farina; musician, rhythm guitarist

1943 Bobby Vee (Velline); singer

1944 Jill Clayburgh; actress

1945 Michael J. Smith; Space Shuttle pilot

1946 Don Schollander; Olympic Hall of Famer, swimming

1948 Perry King; actor

1953 Merrill Osmond; singer

1954 Jane Campion; film director

1961 Isiah Thomas; basketball

1963 Al Lee Toon, Jr.; football

1963 Michael Waltrip; American race car driver

1967 Turbo B (Durron Maurice Butler); singer

1975 Johnny Galecki; actor

1982 Kirsten Dunst; actress

1984 Shawn Daivari; American wrestler and manager

EVENTS FOR APRIL 30th

1492 – Spain gave Christopher Columbus his commission of exploration.

1789 – George Washington took the oath of office on the balcony of Federal Hall on Wall Street in New York City and became the first elected President of the United States.

1803 - The United States purchased the Louisiana Territory from France for $15 million, more than doubling the size of the young nation.

Federal Hall, Seat of Congress. 1790 copper engraving by A. Doolittle, depicting Washington's April 30, 1789 inauguration. Public domain.

1804 – The term "shrapnel," named after the British soldier Henry Shrapnel, was used for the first time in warfare by the British against the Dutch in Suriname, South America.

1812 - Louisiana joined the United States as the 18th state.

1889 - The first national holiday in the United States was celebrated when The U.S. observed the centennial of George Washington's inauguration.

1900 – Hawaii became a territory of the United States, with Sanford B. Dole as governor.

1900 – Train engineer, Casey Jones, was killed when trying to save the *Cannonball Express*.

1904 – The Louisiana Purchase Exposition World's Fair (a.k.a. St. Louis World's Fair, 1904) opened in St. Louis, Missouri.

1938 – The animated cartoon short *Porky's Hare Hunt* debuted in

Portrait of "The Brave Engineer": John Luther "Casey" Jones. Public domain.

movie theaters, introducing Happy Rabbit (who would later be called Bugs Bunny), and Porky Pig.

1939 – The 1939-40 New York World's Fair opened with 206,000 people in attendance. That leads us directly to the next entry . . .

1939 – NBC inaugurated its regularly scheduled television service in New York City, broadcasting President Franklin D. Roosevelt's N.Y. World's Fair opening day ceremonial address.

1939 - The first railroad car equipped with fluorescent lights was put into service. The train car was known as the "General Pershing Zephyr."

1939 - Baseball's "Iron Horse," Lou Gehrig, played his last game with the New York Yankees.

1945 - Arthur Godfrey began his CBS radio morning show which was aptly titled *Arthur Godfrey Time*.

1945 - Adolf Hitler and his wife, Eva Braun, committed suicide in his underground bunker in Berlin after having been married for only one day. Meanwhile, Soviet soldiers raised the Victory Banner over the Reichstag building in Berlin.

Hoover Dam in a historic photo taken by Ansel Adams. Photo provided by the United States National Archives and Records Administration.

1947 – Maps had to be changed once again, as Boulder Dam was changed back to its original name, Hoover Dam.

1956 – Former Vice President and Senator Alben Barkley died during a speech in Virginia. He collapsed after he said, "I would rather be a servant in the house of the lord than sit in the seats of the mighty."

1964 – Beginning today, TV sets would be drastically different after a ruling by the FCC stating that all TVs should be equipped to receive both VHF channels (2-13) and the new UHF channels (14-83).

1966 - Regular hovercraft service began over the English Channel (it was discontinued in 2000 due to the Channel Tunnel).

1969 - The Fifth Dimension was awarded a gold single for "Aquarius/Let the Sunshine In."

1973 – In the midst of the Watergate Scandal U.S. President Richard Nixon announced that top White House aids H.R. Haldeman, John Ehrlichman and others had resigned.

1975 - In South Vietnam, President Minh announced an unconditional surrender to the Vietcong.

1988 – Her Majesty Queen Elizabeth II officially opened World Expo '88 in Brisbane, Australia.

1988 - Celine Dion won the Eurovision Song Contest for Switzerland with the song "Ne Partez Pas Sans Moi."

1990 - American hostage Frank Reed was freed in Lebanon after nearly four years in the hands of pro-Iranian kidnappers.

1992 - Patti Davis, daughter of former-president Ronald and Nancy Reagan, released her book *The Way I See It*.

1993 – Tennis star Monica Seles was stabbed in the back by an obsessed fan of rival Steffi Graf at a tournament in Hamburg, Germany.

1994 - Formula One driver Roland Ratzenberger was killed when his car crashed into a wall while qualifying for the 1994 San Marino Grand Prix.

1995 – U.S. President Bill Clinton became the first President to visit Northern Ireland.

1997 - In a widely publicized episode of the ABC sitcom *Ellen*, TV character Ellen Morgan (played by Ellen DeGeneres) announced that she was gay.

1999 – Cambodia joined the Association of Southeast Asian Nations (ASEAN), bringing the total members to ten.

2001 – *The Mitchell Report* on the Arab-Israeli conflict was published.

2002 – A referendum in Pakistan overwhelmingly approved the Presidency of Pervez Musharraf for another five years.

2004 – U.S. media released graphic photos of American soldiers abusing and sexually humiliating Iraqi prisoners at Abu Ghraib prison.

2008 – Two skeletal remains found near Ekaterinburg, Russia, were confirmed by Russian scientists to be the remains of Alexei Nikolaevich, Tsesarevich (heir apparent) of Russia, and one of his sisters.

2009 – The Chrysler automobile company filed for Chapter 11 bankruptcy.

2010 – Hailed as the largest World's Fair in history, Expo 2010 opened in Shangai, China.

Attributions

Assigning attributions to each morsel of information in a work such as this is, to say the least, a daunting task. True enough, the Internet played a role in research, but it wasn't the only source of information.

At the time of this writing, the word "trivia" was entered into the "search string" on Google. In less than a second, the search engine returned 107 *million* results! To have used nothing but the Internet to confirm these pieces of information would have taken countless hours to churn out ounces of data laced with pounds of errors. A casual comparison between the trivia-based websites will reveal that much of the information had been copied word-for-word from one site to the next. Because of the large number of trivia sites, it is safe to assume that much of the data was copied without verification. The end result was a collection of inaccuracies that were passed from source to source like a harmful virus spreading from host to host.

So, is a claim being made here that every sentence of information in this book is accurate? Yes… to a point. If a statement found was reflected only within trivia, unsupported, or unverifiable sites, it was not included in this work. The only data in this collection are those that could be found in other sources besides trivia sites and, in many cases, external references such as books, magazines, etc.

And then there are the events that occurred to which we were all witness, either through the media or by first-hand experience. These are the best because they are the most reliable.

Even though research has been done to confirm everything found within these covers, the reader is urged to use them at his or her own risk. This book should not be taken as the final word for serious research, but rather a simple companion for light reading, designed to cause a reader to proclaim, "*I'll be darned.*" Use this for conversations at work, dinner table discussions, or for icebreakers. But for serious, detailed research, go to the library.

That being said, here is a list of sources used to compile data for *The Book of April*:

WEB SITES

http://articles.latimes.com

http://www.britannica.com

http://www.cbsnews.com

http://www.culturalcatholic.com

http://www.dickhaymes.com/

http://www.gibson.net

http://www.history.com/

http://www.imdb.com

http://www.kinghussein.gov.jo/

http://www.kipnotes.com/

http://www.nytimes.com

http://www.people.com

http://www.riaa.com/

http://www.time.com

http://www.wikipedia.org/

BOOKS AND PUBLICATIONS

"Good Night, Chet": a Biography of Chet Huntley by Lyle Johnston (book)

Alcalde, The May 2005 (magazine)

American Political Leaders by Richard L. Wilson

American Rebel: The Life of Clint Eastwood by Marc Eliot (book)

Babe Ruth: One of Baseball's Greatest by Guernsey Van Riper

Baseball Digest Jan 2002

Baseball Digest Jul 1964

Big Book of Jewish Baseball: An Illustrated Encyclopedia & Anecdotal History, The by Peter S. Horvitz, Joachim Horvitz

Billboard Apr 20, 1985 (magazine)

Billboard Dec 15, 1984 (magazine)

Blood Evidence: How DNA Is Revolutionizing the Way We Solve Crimes by Henry C. Lee, Frank Tirnady (book)

Bob Dylan: Performing Artist, 1960-1973: the Early Years by Paul Williams

Bowery Boys: Street Corner Radicals and the Politics of Rebellion, The by Peter Adams

Bulletin - United States National Museum, Issues 115-119 by United States National Museum, Smithsonian Institution, United States. Dept. of the Interior (bulletin)

Burlington's Zephyrs by Karl R. Zimmerman

Charting the Times of Your Life by Gary Goldschneider

Chase's Calendar of Events, 2011 Edition by Editors of Chase's Calendar of Events

Civil War America, 1850 to 1875 by Richard F. Selcer

Cold War Frontiers in the Asia-Pacific by Kimie Hara

Collective Conflict Management and Changing World Politics by Joseph Lepgold, Thomas George Weiss

Complete Idiot's Guide To Understanding Iraq, The by Joseph Tragert

Counterterrorism Handbook: Tactics, Procedures, and Techniques, The by Frank Bolz, Kenneth J. Dudonis, David P. Schulz

Cradle Days of New York: (1609-1825) by Hugh Entwistle McAtamney

Creating Country Music: Fabricating Authenticity by Richard A. Peterson

Dixon and Amburn Family History: With Allied Family Sketches of East Tennessee by Shelia Steele Hunt

Duke Ellington: Jazz Composer by Judy Monroe

Earthquakes In Human History: the Far-Reaching Effects of Seismic Disruptions by Jelle Zeilinga de Boer, Donald Theodore Sanders

Eleanor Roosevelt and the Media: a Public Quest for Self-Fulfillment by Maurine Hoffman Beasley

Encyclopedia of Social Reform, The edited by William Dwight Porter Bliss

Encyclopedia of Television by Horace Newcomb, Museum of Broadcast Communications

Famous First Facts About American Politics by Steven Anzovin and Janet Podell

Firsts: Origins of Everyday Things That Changed the World by Wilson Casey

Golden Arches East: McDonald's in East Asia by James L. Watson

Granite Monthly, The Volume 28 edited by Henry Harrison Metcalf, John Norris McClintock (magazine)

Guinness Book of Sports Records, The

Hank Aaron, Baseball Player by Michael Benson

Harry Reasoner: a Life in the News by Douglass K. Daniel

High-Efficient Low-Cost Photovoltaics: Recent Developments by Vesselinka Petrova-Koch

Hollywood Songsters: Garland to O'Connor by James Robert Parish, Michael R. Pitts

Improbable First Century of Cosmopolitan Magazine, The by James Landers

Inner Solar System: The Sun, Mercury, Venus, Earth, and Mars, The by Britannica Educational Publishing

Iraq by Angelia L. Mance

Lend Me Your Ears: Great Speeches in History by William Safire

Lives of the Popes: Illustrated Biographies of Every Pope From St Peter to the Present by Michael J. Walsh

Louisville By James Anderson, Donna Neary

Magical Life of Marshall Brodien, The by John A. Moehring

Mario Andretti by G. S. Prentzas

Milwaukee Bucks by Tom Peterson

Money Matrix of the New World Order, The by Phillip Tilley

Motion Picture in its Economic and Social Aspects, The by Gordon S. Watkins

New Dickson Baseball Dictionary, The by Paul Dickson

New International Encyclopædia, Volume 17, The edited by Daniel Coit Gilman, Harry Thurston Peck, Frank Moore Colby

New York City Mayors by Ralph J. Caliendo

Notes Toward a History of the American Newspaper by William Nelson

Now You Know Big Book of Sports by Doug Lennox

On the Air: the Encyclopedia of Old-Time Radio by John Dunning

Pilot's Handbook of Aeronautical Knowledge edited by Federal Aviation Administration

Political Commentators in the United States in the 20ᵗʰ Century by Dan D. Nimmo, Chevelle Newsome

Potter's American Monthly, Volume 3 (periodical)

Rise and Fall of the Third Reich: a History of Nazi Germany, The by William L. Shirer

Routledge guide to Broadway, The by Ken Bloom

Sanctioning Iran: Anatomy of a Failed Policy by Hossein Alikhani

Scientific American, Volume 2 by Making of America Project

Station to Station: the History of Rock 'n' Roll On Television by Marc Weingarten

Television and National Sport: the United States and Britain by Joan Mary Chandler

Terrorism: Avoidance and Survival by Chester L. Quarles

Third City: Chicago and American Urbanism, The by Larry Bennett

Universe, The by Educational Publishing Britannica Educational Publishing, Erik Gregersen

When I'm bad, I'm better: Mae West, Sex, and American Entertainment by Marybeth Hamilton

Women of Science: Righting the Record by Gabriele Kass-Simon

Worldwalk by Steven M Newman

Yogi Berra: An American Original by New York Daily News

Your Birthday Sign Through Time: A Chronicle of the Forces That Shape Your Destiny by Skye Alexander, Rochelle Gordon, Nadia Stieglitz

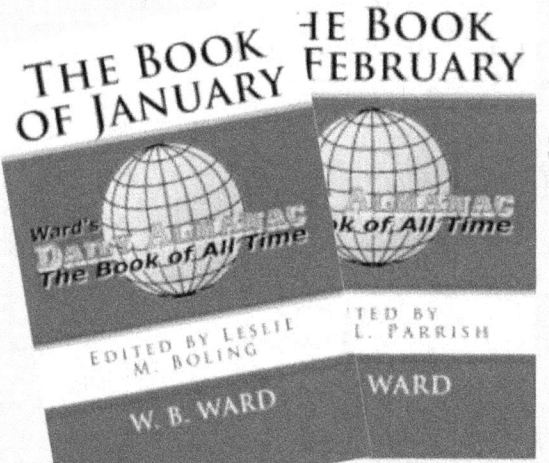

www.ingramcontent.com/pod-product-compliance
Lightning Source LLC
Chambersburg PA
CBHW081347280526
45788CB00009B/2796